THE MICROGUIDE TO
PROCESS MODELING IN BPMN

THE MICROGUIDE TO PROCESS MODELING IN BPMN

TOM DEBEVOISE
TIPPING POINT SOLUTIONS, INCORPORATED

AND

RICK GENEVA
INTALIO SOFTWARE, INCORPORATED

TIPPING POINT SOLUTIONS, INCORPORATED
LEXINGTON, VIRGINIA

The MicroGuide to Process Modeling in BPMN

These books are widely used by corporations and government agencies for training. The publisher offers discounts on this book when ordered in bulk quantities. For more information contact booksurge publications (www.booksurge.com) and query on title or ISBN.

ISBN: 978-1-4196-9310-6

Library of Congress Control Number: 2008902478

Composition and book design by TIPS Technical Publishing, Inc.

Cover design by Russell Halsted

This book is dedicated to all the business analysts who work to improve their firms' processes. In so doing, they improve everyone's experience.

—Tom Debevoise

CONTENTS

FOREWORD

Don't let the title fool you: Tom and Rick's *MicroGuide to Process Modeling in BPMN* is nothing but a major contribution to the field of Business Process Modeling. In fact, thanks to numerous real world scenarios, this work is nothing short of one of the best introductions to Business Process Management that has been published so far. It covers most aspects of the Business Process Modeling Notation (BPMN) in a clear and concise manner, yet sheds lights on some of the most powerful elements of this standard notation—many of which are simply ignored by other publications. BPM is one of the most overused acronyms currently branded by IT vendors and business consultants alike. It is also one of the disciplines least understood by customers due to lack of proper reference materials. *The MicroGuide to Process Modeling in BPMN* is a fantastic step toward a much needed clarification, and a tool that should benefit all BPM practitioners tremendously.

—Ismael Chang Ghalimi
CEO Intalio

PREFACE

A PUBLISHING IDEA:
THE COMPLETE MICROGUIDE

Introducing the Microguide

In the December 2007 issue of the *Economist*, I read that Harvard Business Press has begun publishing small books of roughly 100 pages in length. I rejoiced at this idea! For years it seemed that overstuffed business and technical books that have a notoriously short shelf life have been foisted on readers. And it's no coincidence that professionals in business and technology have very little time to read huge texts with mountains of theory and analysis on any topic, let alone that which they need in their daily work.

When I read that smaller, more one-topic books were becoming popular, I decided that the Information Technology (IT) industry was a perfect target for books like this. How much more manageable it would be to pick up a 125-page book on a technical issue—one that you could easily finish in a day or two, or even on a long plane flight! This seemed to me to be the next big hit in IT publishing, and I have lots of information that I can capture in 100-120 pages.

So, in the spirit of providing the most current information on one specific topic in one convenient place, this book communicates the prevailing wisdom on process modeling in a brief, concise way. Some of the lessons we have learned about process modeling are

- Folks often bring preconceived notions about process modeling to our classes and consulting engagements.
- BPMN is not workflow modeling, flowcharts, XML Process Definition Language (XPDL), or Unified Modeling Language (UML). The approach is different and must be learned.

- BPMN is not a "requirements modeling" tool. It is designed to build executable processes.
- Every statement in your business conversations, use cases, and technical documents should not become BPMN shapes. For instance, a truth table should not become a bunch of BPMN boxes and diamonds.
- BPMN is not a programming language. You cannot reverse-engineer your PL/SQL, COBOL or BPEL into BPMN.

Because this is a MicroGuide, there is no need to review the history of process management, starting with Adam Smith's pin factory and projecting to communications with other civilizations. There is no need to recite the history of computing, starting with the abacus and projecting to cybernetic networks. There is also no need to proclaim a revolution of New World business and technical nirvana solved by business processes and/or decision management.

It is easy to be confused when you start building diagrams in BPMN. When execution is the goal, it is easy for a modeling team's important, early efforts to be lost. Consultants and firms often use BPMN as a replacement for requirements specifications. This approach is not the aim of BPMN and the BPM movement. BPMN progressively employs a process with information flowing from the earliest strategic phases though final integration of specifications.

BPMN should not be used to build a "requirements specification" to outsource process implementation. If your firm does this, it will lose valuable proprietary knowledge. You will also lose business agility. Subject matter experts and process analysts maintain process integrity by changing BPMN shapes, business rules, and data elements, and redeploying the process. Some firms have composed processes in BPMN and outsourced their maintenance. Subsequently, they create the necessary Corporate Maturity Model Integration (CMMI) change documents. This is patently ridiculous.

The Author's Business Model

We have written this book to provide a service to you, the reader. The service is a rapid understanding of the topic of business process modeling in BPMN. To build on this understanding, Rick Geneva and I drew on our personal experiences and the experiences of our clients, peers, and students.

As a writer, publishing a book is also a marketing tool for my services—training and consulting. These services are explained and available on *www.tomdebevoise.com/training* and *www.BPMCertifiedExpert.com*.

Also, you can join my mailing list at these locations. In exchange for your contact information, we will provide BPMN modeling examples and information.

Rick's motivation for writing this book began in 2000 while working as a software architect for a large enterprise. First, there was frustration—four months of development just to transfer one text field to a webpage. Then there was an epiphany—the outdated software development methodologies and inadequate process documentation techniques of the time are actually the culprit!

Rick has been working with Business Process Management (BPM) and Service-Oriented Architecture (SOA) concepts since 2001, before these concepts were an accepted formal practice. Rick has worked for several BPM vendors. In 2007, he joined Intalio (*www.intalio.com*) as a process expert, which is a hybrid role of both business analyst and IT architect. You can read more about Rick at *www.rickgeneva.com* and his process modeling blog at *www.process-modeling.com*.

Process Modeling Framework (PMF)

The Process Modeling Framework (PMF) is an idealized practice that defines increasing details for process models and reveals those details. PMF was developed through numerous consulting engagements over several years. Patterns were observed for both BPMN process models and interactions between departments within an organization. These patterns were then formalized into the PMF.

Rick and I do not claim to "own" the PMF. Currently, the PMF is not a commercially available, licensed methodology. Yet, when you start modeling a project's processes, you should start with a hierarchy of processes models. These start with core business models for executives and their line of business managers. The models end with detailed service models that provide important technical details. The precise levels are suggested, not compulsory.

This book is written to explain how to model processes in BPMN with any methodology. Clearly, BPMN presets a new, more succinct approach to digitizing the modeling process.

—Tom Debevoise
Spring, 2008

CHAPTER 1

INTRODUCTION

BPMN BACKGROUND

With over fifty implementations listed, Business Process Modeling Notation (BPMN) is an increasingly successful Object Management Group (OMG) standard. Yet, BPMN is more than a mere standard; it is a powerful, concise modeling tool. This chapter outlines the principles that underpin modeling processes in BPMN. We also explain some of the benefits of BPMN.

This chapter introduces a Process Modeling Framework (PMF). A by-product of years of working with BPMN process modeling, the PMF outlines a method that you can progressively adapt to your needs. The PMF proscribes progressively detailed process diagrams and builds models from the earliest strategy phase to the goal—execution. In short, there are no wasted efforts.

BPMN: The Foundation for Understandable Models

The designers of BPMN use new principles to improve the output of process modelers. Understanding the benefits on BPMN is simple.

BPMN engines use BPMN to build more accurate and organic process descriptions than older approaches to process and workflow modeling. In the past, most workflow software used a form of "Petri-nets." A Petri-net graphically depicts the structure of a set of distributed processes. It uses mathematical ideas, including place nodes, transition nodes, and directed arcs. Figure 1–1 presents an old style of processes in a contracting system.

With a BPMN approach, solutions to business problems appear through more familiar concepts. Processes in BPMN show high-level and low-level details in a single diagram. This is a technical and documentation improvement over Petri-nets. As shown in Figure 1–2, a BPMN diagram shows timing as well as responsibility—who does what, when they do it, and how it is done relative to

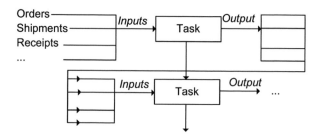

Figure 1–1   *A process in workflow (Petri-net) format.*

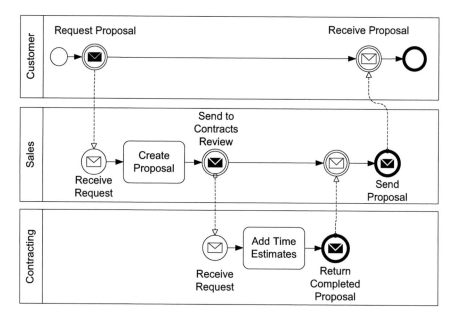

Figure 1–2   *BPMN diagram showing timeline, responsibilities, and activity synchronization.*

other process participants. Each participant has their own view of the process and the data.

Workflow data models do not permit all activities to have access to process data. In Figure 1–3, a purchase request generated at the "Receive Order" step is not available to those responsible for the "Ship Order" step unless it is explicitly passed through the "Process Order" step. The data flow and sequence flow are the same.

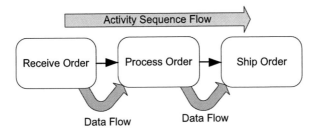

Figure 1–3   *The Legacy workflow data processing model.*

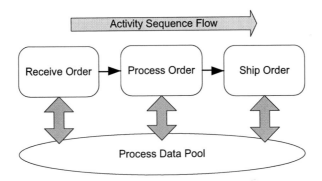

Figure 1–4   *Pi-Calculus processing model.*

In contrast, the BPMN approach allows activities access to process data at any point in the processes activity chain. All process data is organized in a common pool, and the sequence flow and data flow are independent. For instance, in Figure 1–4, a purchase order might be output at the Receive Order step and an invoice might be output at the Process Order step. When the process reaches the Ship Order activity, the purchase order and invoice are available without explicitly passing data.

Through BPMN, Pi-Calculus is the theoretical basis for creating industry-supported solutions to business problems. Another vision of the BPM movement is the exchange of processes among partners. Currently, a theoretically sound way to exchange processes in a lengthy transaction is with systems that use Pi-Calculus engines. As we will discover in the coming chapters, Pi-Calculus solves patterns that solve complicated problems. So, BPM notation is only a starting point. The outcome of using BPMN is a simpler and more natural approach to modeling processes.

DEFINITIONS

In today's BPM industry, terms such as "business process" or "business rules" have many definitions. We have selected definitions that help you model processes in BPMN. You should understand the following basic definitions.

Business Process Defined

A business process is a sequence of activities that carry out a business goal. More accurately, and from the viewpoint of BPMN,

> *A business process is a flow of decision-coordinated activities, conducted by participants and acting on data, information, and knowledge that reach a goal.*

This definition arises from a compendium of BPM literature and the business rules community. It concisely defines

- The end state of process design
- The design choices of BPMN shapes
- The role of business rules
- Knowledge-based control of process relationships with economic conditions

Next, we define the important ideas of the definition:

- An event (shown by a circle shape) is a message, indicator, announcement, or something similar that represents that an instance has happened and has been registered.
- A flow (shown by lines and arrows) is a motion of data from shape to shape. There are two types of flows in a business process—a sequence and a message. Flows can move from event to event, activity to activity, and activity to event.
- Data consists of structured information, owned by a business process. Business processes can also pass on unstructured documents.
- Knowledge is information applied to problem-solving. Knowledge adapts the process to conditions beyond the normal operating conditions.
- A business decision is one or more business rules applied to process information.
- An activity (shown by a rounded rectangle) is a task that is performed by a process participant.

- A participant (shown by a horizontal or vertical lane) is any resource that is involved in a business process—be it a human person, a group of people, a system, or another process.

The process goal is started, for example, when a customer fills out an order form. You would not consider it complete until the interface program posts the order to the Enterprise Resource Planning (ERP).

These ideas are critical to the proper design of a decision-directed process. Your process analysts will need to identify these within "business conversations." One goal of this book is to explain how to parse the words. Ideally, the process modeling framework directs your process modeling group's conversations.

Business Process Management

Business Process Management (BPM) is the identification, understanding, and management of business processes that support a firm's business model. The processes link decisions with people and systems in and across organizations. Ideally, processes support a business model that adapts to changes in economics, customer preferences, and best practices. More often, short-term organizational needs create processes. The scope of these process project portfolios is driven by low performance and disruptions. Processes that cannot adapt to changing economic operating conditions will have a short lifespan.

BPM 2.0

Several visionary vendors are innovating in the BPM space by promoting "code-free" approaches to developing business processes. The aim is to increase the simplicity and transparency of the artifacts by

- Reducing software programming work
- Increasing the use of visual coding techniques, especially BPMN

BPMN is a critical standard for BPM 2.0.

Business Rules Defined

A business rule is a mediator of information in computer systems for decision-making process participants such as managers, employees, and salespeople. More accurately and from the viewpoint of the business process,

> *A business rule is an atomic logic step that uses data and knowledge to evaluate part of a proposition about a process decision.*

The business rule "meets" the process through the decision. So, business rules decide with information. When you change the business rule, you change the decision outcome. A business rule can be a policy, a constraint, or a regulatory requirement. Think of a truth table where condition values in the table's columns match the conclusion. The truth table could filter the information needed to decide whether to extend credit to a customer. Each row in the truth table is a business rule. The business rule is not the decision—it is a logical condition of the decision.

Business Rules Approach Defined

The business rules approach is a design technique for formalizing an enterprise's critical rules in a language that the manager and technologist understand. The language is simple for business analysts to create and combine with business process approaches. Analysts and subject matter experts gather business rules with the business rules approach. We will also cover business rules in the chapter on requirements. In the middle phases of the process modeling framework, analysts and subject matter experts discover business rules that support process decisions. Business rules begin with a glossary and an unambiguous statement of what a business does with information to decide a proposition (business language). Analysts form a formal statement of the rule from the business language.

Process Decisions

Business processes use business rules in making decisions. Decisions are settled with process data evaluated by business rules engines. When parsing a formal statement of a business rule, technical activities define the terms, translations, or transformations of the rule. The outcome is metadata that describes a decision with a truth table or a stepwise formatted business rule. The result is a precise definition of the decision machinery. Because the definition is precise, firms improve process decisions with confidence.

Decision Management Defined

From the perspective of BPM, a decision is a judgment about a business term or idea. In their book *Smart Enough Systems*, Taylor and Raden define a business decision as applying business rules to an unresolved business issue. We define the business decision as a determination about a business term or concept. Decision management, then, is the practice of

- Identifying decisions within business processes—digitized or otherwise
- Integrating the decisions into services used by processes
- Precisely and unambiguously representing and populating a decision model structure with individual business rules

The business rules should be important to (and aligned with) the business during an operating period. The business rules approach empowers organizations to change business rules to adjust to their needs. Therefore, business processes are more powerful when they are designed with a decision-management approach. We call these "decision-directed processes." With decision management, decisions become strategic assets of a firm. As with any asset, their value to the firm is quantifiable and understood.

The Service-Oriented Architecture (SOA) provides a technical platform for decision services. In SOA services, decision services are published contracts with well-defined terms, interfaces, and exception handling.

An advanced form of decision management is known as Enterprise Decision Management (EDM). Taylor and Raden define EDM as a

> systematic approach to automating and improving operational business decisions. Enterprise Decision Management aims to increase the precision, consistency, and agility of these decisions while reducing the time taken to decide and the cost of the decision.

EDM extends decision management by automating the basis for business rule changes and predicting the outcome of the changes. Advanced EDM architectures can adjust business rules to fine-tune decisions. EDM offers an approach to some of any firm's most challenging problems.

BPMN CONCEPTS

The Building Blocks of the Foundation

To create a proper BPMN diagram, you need to grasp the BPMN concepts we introduced in the definitions. If you jump ahead to the section on BPMN shapes, you might create workflow-style diagrams with BPMN. As James Chang has pointed out, traditional or functional work management suffers from a lack of end-to-end focus. It is not only the shapes that make the BPMN diagram different. BPMN expresses processes in a Pi-Calculus way. In a concise way, BPMN shapes draw up the essence of a business process.

Some of these concepts are part of the definitions of business process: an **event**-activated **flow** of decision-coordinated **activities**, conducted by **participants** and acting on **data**, information, and knowledge that achieve a goal. The five other concepts are divisions of these.

Participant

Designers of the BPMN notation have founded the process on the basis of the participant. A participant is an actor or a person that interacts in a process. The actor includes any human, digital, or virtual resource that is involved in a business process. Participants can include people, systems, machines, other processes, groups of people, and groups of systems.

Processes can also be participants. From a modeling perspective, a process is treated just like another participant. Sometimes, processes interact with each other.

Contract receipting is a good example: the Inventory Receipt process hands off to... the Inventory Inspection process, which hands off to... the Invoicing process, which hands off to... the Account Payable process.

Examples of participants include:

People Participants

- Inventory receipt clerk inspecting the order
- Customer Service Representative answering a request
- Employee filling out a requisition
- Patient in a hospital
- Manager approving a requisition
- Technician restoring a disk drive
- A loan officer reviewing an application

System Participants

- Oracle Financials, JD Edwards, SAP, Peoplesoft
- Oracle, MySQL, DB2 database server
- ILog, OpenLexicon, Fair Isaac, rules engine
- A telephony queuing switch
- A Web service
- An application server (an EJB or method)
- A custom-built User Interface (UI)
- An enterprise service business, message broker (an MQ-Series or Tuxedo queue)

System participants might also be "roles." A role is a logical grouping of people and systems that perform a general work category in the process diagram context. People and systems can have different roles. Roles rarely mix people and systems. For example, a person enters data and a system receives and processes the data. Although people and systems perform similar work, the role recognizes a division of responsibility within a business process.

Scope Context

A "scope" is a logical container or a placeholder of changing information. By default, all processes have a hierarchy of scope context. At the top is "business process scope," which contains everything in the process. In the scope of the entire (top) process, a business objective, with well-defined start and end points, exists for the entire process. More refined scopes arise as you break the diagram down into smaller sections with more specific participant (or data) details. Therefore, a logical division of activities and data arises as we add details to our diagram.

Activity

An "activity" is work the participant performs with business processes. In the simplest form, the activity can be atomic or nonatomic (a compound). Processes and subprocesses are compound activities. In BPMN, the types of process activities include tasks and subprocesses.

The task is the atomic activity. Because it is atomic, there are no further details. The subprocess is a compound activity that might contain other activities. An activity can be manual, as a human participant completes the activity, or it might be automated by a system participant. As defined, the activity is a core part of the business process.

Examples of activities include

- Inspecting material delivery
- Restoring a server
- Completing contract requisition
- Reviewing and approving a requisition
- Reviewing load application

Flow

"Flow" is the order (and data) in which the activities or process steps are performed. Multiple flows might occur within multiple participant roles. The correct BPMN shape defines how flows can be sequenced. Sequences might run sequentially or in parallel. There are two types of flows in a BPMN diagram:

- *Sequence*—defines the order in which activities are performed for any given process participant. Sequence flow never occurs *between* participants.
- *Message*—defines the flow of information and messages between participants within a process. Messages never occur within the same participant.

Transition

A "transition" describes the hand off between activities. A transition is more specific than a connection from one process step to the next. Transition means that one activity has stopped, and another has started. They are part of the scope of the process, where scope is a snapshot of the process instance data. If each task has a scope, then the scope transitions from one activity to the next. A transition sequence might simultaneously split into many paths. Overall, a transition recognizes that one activity has stopped and that others have started.

Transition never occurs between multiple participants. Imagine a work area with people and workstations for each person's activities (tasks). Participants walk about unaided performing various tasks. As each task is completed, the person transitions to the next task at another workstation. While performing these tasks, participants collect more information and take it to the next workstation, where they may use the information to decide the next task. Here, participants have not communicated with anyone else. Any communication is an interaction, not a transition.

Interaction

Communication between participants takes place with "interactions." Interactions occur between two or more participants in the form of messages. Interactions never occur from one participant back to itself. Note: a flow from one participant back to itself is an activity transition, not an interaction.

Consider the workstation scenario from the transition discussion. Now imagine a work area full of people performing tasks. Participants communicate and ask for help. They might say, "I need to know the order number for...." Other participants' tasks may complete and forward a document. Other tasks may need an introduction, a handshake, an exchange of information, and a farewell. All these are forms of interactions. As we start to create BPMN diagrams, you will see how this concept applies to your business processes.

Imagine a BPMN diagram of a manual process involving two people communicating. In BPMN, a message is an exchange between those people, including written, verbal, or any other form of communication. In another example, two computer systems communicate in an automated process. A message occurs each time the participants send and receive data and information. An interaction may include a data request and an acknowledgement message.

Event

An "event" marks a change in the state of conditions in a process. A process event defines a point where the process is either started, stopped, halted, or continued. Events might direct a process from the original flow into an alternate path. Importantly, events define occurring activities "of interest." Normally, participant actions, choices, or activities define or create events. An empty event has undefined criteria.

Examples of events include

- Contract order submitted
- Database unavailable
- Contract requisition completed
- Requisition rejected
- Load application received

Data

There is only one shape in BPMN for "data," yet data is a critical part of the business process. All business processes own structured information. This might include business forms, interface data elements, and data from screens. Process activities manipulate data, and sequence flows map the attributes. Processes communicate with data across sequence flows and message flows.

To reach a process decision, business rules evaluate data values. Therefore, business rules use the values from the fields in the structured information. The business rules approach defines a vocabulary for this information.

Each process instance holds a unique collection of data. Each process participant owns information—people provide knowledge, systems have data. The process decisions judge or decide and direct the flow of the process. Business rules direct the decisions. The decision controls the flow and acts on the data. Through interactions with others, process participants gather information. For instance,

- An ordering assistant can tell her manager which vendors provide a product.
- An ERP contracting application can report vendor information created by another participant.

Processes contribute to the data stream. Decisions also create and manipulate data. For example, a decision may decide what price to apply to an item on a requisition. This is known as a transformation.

Data elements arise from

- Business process, design, and the progressive refinements of the design
- Business rules, concepts, guidelines
- Metrics, aggregate performance
- Interaction between participants

Sources of data elements include

- Activity requirements
- Paper documents such as business forms or signed agreements
- Electronic documents such as fax, email, or PDFs
- ERP transaction elements
- Computations for data needed in decisions

PROCESS ARCHETYPES

The American Heritage dictionary defines an archetype as "an original model or type after which similar category members are patterned; a prototype." Processes archetypes are patterns of organizational behavior that managers set up about lines of businesses. They have organically spread in the modern worlds of business and government. Business models—frameworks for creating value—use process archetypes to define the operating characteristics and as a common language. Process improvements inspire innovation.

You might recall many different processes you have worked with. With the process concepts we have defined, we can discuss some classic types of processes that might occur in your firm. Also, these processes become more descriptive and familiar in BPMN. For instance, items in an inventory process own a process instance. That is, if there is a physical item in the store, warehouse, or employee truck, you can find it in a process instance. A purchase order in a BPMN process is more than a database table. It is a model of all the phases, permutations, and errors that the "purchase order" can experience. Many technical books mention the order-to-cash process. I will mention three processes that are familiar, yet we hope not overused.

BPMN shapes should be labeled with the activities, events and participants of your organization. If your process tracks flower deliveries, then the process should have a truck delivering flowers to a customer. We will use these process archetypes in the chapters of this book, so it is useful to briefly describe them.

Inventory Management

Inventory management processes manage and control inventory at various stock points in a firm's value chain. Inventory management processes differ for bulk and discrete items. Bulk inventory might include liquids such as fuels, chemicals, and water. Other bulk items include solids such as grain or gasses such as propane. Discrete items are usually managed at an individual level.

For decades firms have sought to optimize or cut out inventory subprocesses. Firms use innovation frameworks such as Lean or Just-In-Time (JIT) inventory. For all these innovations, inventory management processes still exist. Innovative accounting practices, such as pay-on-receipt, reduce inventory management's wasteful steps. Inventory must be shelved in retail stores, received into warehouses or factory bins, and distributed.

Inventory Subprocesses

At a high level, inventory subprocesses might include

- ERP—the ERP systems hold inventory account balances.
- Issues—customers receive inventory from a stock point.
- Returns—customers return unneeded stock or stock not meeting agreed standards.
- Receipts—items that are received from a firm's vendors and trading partners are receipts. Items received from another stock point might be another subprocess (shipment receipt).
- Inspections—in generally accepted accounting practices, items are not considered part of the inventory until they are inspected.
- Shipments—most inventory processes define a shipment as moving inventory from stock-point to stock-point within a firm. Valuable inventory might require the use of an employee's vehicle as a stock-point.
- Item processes—in BPMN you might create a process instance for each item in your stock. The other processes such as issue, returns, shipment and receipt act on the individual items.
- Inventory Reconciliation—inventory processes identify the net of issues, returns, shipments, and receipts. The difference is the unexplained gain or loss.

Inventory Participants

At a high level, inventory participants might include

- Stock clerks—personnel that receive and manage physical inventory.
- Quality inspectors—personnel that inspect physical inventory.
- Contract systems (see Maintenance Manangement Participants)— systems that create a purchase of inventory from a vendor or trading partner.
- Laboratory systems—systems that use procedures to inspect bulk and discrete items.
- Transportation systems—a firm's systems for sourcing and moving inventory material.
- Quality systems—firms adopt quality methodologies and quality ensure they are carried out.

Inventory Decisions

Inventory processes are a bountiful source of process decisions. Inventory decision might include

- Target Inventory levels—a firm's business model tightly controls the target inventory level. For instance, in Lean manufacturing the goal is to have no inventory backlogs.
- Issues and sales—when and where customers might receive inventory.
- Returns—under what condition might inventory be returned.
- In receipts there are often contracting policies that define when, where and how much inventory can be received from a vendor.
- Inspections—quality policies decide what material is accepted, rejected or downgraded.
- Shipments—transportation rules decide how material is sent.

Maintenance Management

Maintenance management processes manage a firm's long-term assets. Different types of assets drive different approaches to maintenance. Fleet management is a maintenance management process for cars, trucks, and rolling stock. There are maintenance management approaches for real estate. Like the inventory process, discrete items can be managed at an individual level. That is, the process model creates an instance for every maintained item.

Maintenance Management Subprocesses

At a high level, maintenance management processes might include:

- Asset onboarding—similar to an employee onboarding process or the entire life cycle for buying an asset.
- Maintenance—the periodic or acute maintenance of a fixed asset. A firm might own many thousands of asset types that require many different maintenance schedules. Products are also often recalled.
- Operator assignment—employees and contractors assigned a firm's equipment.
- Asset process—each significant, nonincidental item should be an instance of a process.
- Salvage—at the end of its useful life, an asset should be salvaged, recycled, or disposed.

Maintenance Management Participants

At a high level, maintenance management participants might include

- Fleet managers—managers that receive and manage fleets or vehicles.
- Mechanics—personnel that service equipment.
- Contracting systems (see Inventory Participants)—those a firm might purchase or use to maintain long-term assets from vendors.
- Transportation systems—assets might be moved between locations.
- Personnel training systems—assigned personnel are properly trained/certified to use the equipment they are assigned.
- Fuel—for fleet management, the cost of fuel can be huge. Fuel management systems can track and reduce this cost.

Maintenance Management Decisions/ Business Rules

Maintenance management processes decisions might include

- Purchase/lease—should the asset be purchased or leased?
- Certify assets—based on the firm's experience, is this the type of equipment desired?
- Assign/deny the issue of equipment—are employees qualified to use vehicles based on training certifications?
- Salvage/sell—when should the asset be salvaged or sold before the depreciation?

Supplier Relationship Management

Supplier Relationship Management (SRM) processes manage a firm's agreement between trading partners. The type of firm creates different approaches to SRM or contracting processes. Government agencies must follow detailed acquisition regulations. Practices at commercial firms vary from traditional contract agreements to the flyweight practices proscribed by Six Sigma or Lean. Despite a relabeling from contracting to SRM in inventory management, old contract practices can never disappear. Firms may claim to have expelled contracting practices, but the truth is revealed when legal difficulties occur.

SRM Activities and Subprocesses

At a high level, SRM subprocesses might include

- Contract or supplier relationship management establishment including advertising, bidding, and awards. This is called "contract award." Government agencies are often required to perform these steps.
- Supplier certification—using internal and industrial processes to verify that the supplier meets the needs.
- Requisition (order)—most firms consider a requisition to be an internal request for products and services. Contracting applications will source the requisition to a particular contractor and order the products and services. Lean or Agile manufacturing systems lighten and hide the clunky details of this process and build a "pull" system.
- Delivery—the ordered product and service is delivered.
- Receipt and invoice—after the product and service is inspected (see Inventory Decisions), a financial instrument for payment is created.
- Contract change order—the terms and conditions of the requisition are altered.

Participants

At a high level, contract subprocesses might include

- Supplier manager— the person responsible for relationships.
- Requisition officer—person approving or reviewing requisitions and orders.
- Requisition or supply clerk—a person planning the delivery of products and services.
- Transportation systems—when organizations provide transportation for vendor products, a transportation system might be involved.
- Manufacturing systems—if the firm makes products and services, then it requisitions products and services.
- Inventory/inspection—a firm receives tangible products and inspects them.
- Quality systems—either through the inventory system or as a part of the SRM.

SRM Policies and Business Rules

SRM process decisions might include

- Vendor certification/disqualification—deciding which vendors should be certified or disqualified from engaging the firm.
- Sourcing the order—deciding which vendor receives and order.
- Award—awarding a contract might require many business rules.
- Transportation—deciding transportation types for multiple suppliers.

From Archetypes to Digitized Processes: A Process Modeling Framework (PMF)

I hope you recognized one of the process archetypes. Yet how would you move from these short paragraphs towards a digitized model? True corporate processes are notoriously complex and involve thousands of activities and participants. This complexity has amassed over decades of practice. Detecting what is necessary and important is difficult. Therefore, business conversations might take weeks or even months. Fortunately, BPMN is flexible and easily moves from high-level details to the smallest behavior needed for execution. Figure 1–5 presents a concept diagram of PMF.

With the activity types shown in Figure 1–5, the process team creates progressive models for a solution that either carries out or updates a business process. There are three classes of activities: process modeling (BPMN), business rules, and data modeling (XML).

As shown to the left of Figure 1–5, there are four role categories assigned to the activities in the PMF: Executive, Management, Subject Matter Expert (SME), and Technical. Because it is role-based, the PMF simplifies your process team's activities and radically reduces wasteful efforts. The PMF gradually matures your existing process (or use case) modeling methods. By gathering understanding and knowledge from the correct source, PMF creates an efficient focus on process improvement. For instance,

- Directors and managers do not take part in most conversations about businesses rules for decisions.
- Business analysts do not take part in conversations about database service-level agreements.
- Subject matter experts contribute expertise when it is needed and in a natural way.

The outcome of this framework is a decision-directed process. Before we present the PMF, we need to define the important terms of process modeling.

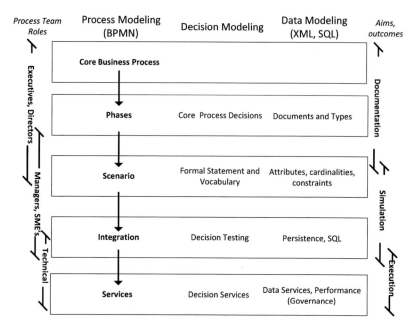

Figure 1–5 *Activities, participants, and objectives of the PMF.*

Warning! If you do not adopt progressive levels, your documents will quickly become unwieldy. With an unstructured approach,

- Your modeling efforts are frustrating and unfocused.
- Your BPMN diagram will be inscrutable to managers.
- You might create too many activities in a single process, adding to the confusion.
- You might add quickly changing business rules to diagrams at the wrong point.
- You might miss the patterns within a larger view of these processes.

The common symptoms of these conditions are design (Joint Application Design (JAD)) sessions with poster-sized "stickies" that run around an entire wall. Such symptoms are overcome by creating processes with the PMF in BPMN. In the spirit of BPM, this process delivers a progression of BPMN diagrams that progressively identify participants, activities, events, and decisions. The diagrams create process definitions. Business rules support decisions and should not be expressed in BPMN. The process also identifies activities that need details for execution. The difference is that you view systems, such as ERP, as providers of services. With PMF, you define how your business uses the services.

The PMF combines business process management and decision management. Collectively, these bring business process design, important SOA services, and other IT parts together in an accurate, repeatable way. The top-level activities in PMF are

- Core process modeling
- Phases of the modeling process
- Scenario modeling in BPMN and business rules
- Integration modeling and business rules implementation
- Modeling for business, system, and decision services

A step-by-step way to foresee the PMF approach is to describe it in a use case—a sequential description of the interaction between actors and a system. The use case describes the behavior of the system for the expected outcome. In a later chapter, we will describe a step-by-step procedure for converting a use case into a process design. Assuming a process modeling project has been selected, the use case for PMF is:

Step One: Core Process Modeling

Top-level management and technical executives create a core business architecture study to define the scope of the process model. Modern approaches, especially Lean methods, might create core processes as a function of value-chain mapping. The core business process contains only the highest-level block diagram (see Figure 1–6). This group only needs to understand a few BPMN shapes. There should be no workflow or integration. For instance, a core business diagram for government contracting might include the following subprocesses:

- Budget
- Advertising
- Contract awards
- Period of performance
- Contract closeout

Core diagrams should include only the major steps of a process, and might include one or two major decisions. For example, in a loans process, things start with an application process, then go into an approval process. If approved, it goes into loan disbursement. If rejected, the loan goes into a notification process. Each time the loan changes state, a new process is used to implement the new phase. The gateway is shown in the core process model because it depicts the critical decision path. All activity prior to this gateway establishes the data to support this decision.

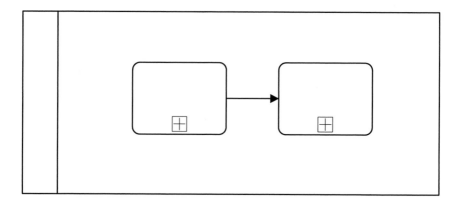

Figure 1–6   *Core diagrams show highest-level conceptual details. The two subprocesses become the subject of the next phase of the PMF—the process phase.*

The core business might define desired future business behavior and "as is" business behavior in two separate diagrams. The outcome of this step is an enterprise- or business-wide core business process.

Step Two: Phases Modeling

For each subprocess in the core business process, Line of Business (LOB) area management and technical leaders identify the phases of the processes in detailed activities and decisions. A precondition is the phases where groups grasp a few more BPMN shapes, yet low-level details, such as the rules that direct the decisions, are left for later phases.

In our government contracting example, the subprocess for a contract award goes through these phases:

- Open bids
- Review responsiveness
- **Decide** on nonresponsiveness
- Notify nonresponsive
- **Decide** on contract award
- Notify contract award and nonaward
- Receive bid protest
- **Decide** protest action
- Award contract

The bold **Decide** identifies process decisions, supported by business rules. The outcome is a process phase model for activity within the core process. The process phase model defines the activities and essential decisions within the process. Decisions are not business rules. They are gateways to different parts of the process.

High-level document types are gathered in the data model of the process phase. In our example, documents include the contract, the award, and the vendor bid. Other sources of document types might include external systems such as SAP iDOCS.

The decision gateways in a phase diagram often act as a filter to optimize resources. For example, if a technical team is needed for a labor estimate, the phase might route sequence flow to the labor estimation process, which is likely a scenario diagram.

It might seem easier to place a human-centric task directly into a phase diagram. As the process matures, however, you will likely find each scenario becoming more complex and easier to manage separately. A phase diagram is rarely reusable in other processes. Key decisions are made here that are not found elsewhere in the process. In contrast, scenario diagrams are usually reusable in multiple-phase diagrams. Therefore, placing direct participant interactions at the phase level might result in duplicating these steps elsewhere.

Step Three: Scenario Modeling and Business Rules

For each subprocess at this level, LOB managers and SMEs identify detailed scenarios and business rules. In scenario modeling, each BPMN diagram is a concise, manageable workflow scenario. As modeling advances, changes can often occur without affecting the rest of the core or phase diagrams. In our government contracting example, the subprocess for the "review responsiveness" part of contract award would include all the needed activities and workflow. There might be many approving organizations involved and more business rules behind the decisions.

In scenario modeling, we detail the interfaces of the processes. That is, the processes output has a modular design and can be reused by other processes.

Even if the project team needs to finish work for execution, the team might simulate these processes. Simulation helps detect and diagnose performance problems before the team finishes the entire project. If more business rules are needed, the project members might hand code sample business rules into dummy subprocesses.

When the team simulates early prototypes, they test the modeling products more thoroughly and in less time. They catch more defects and release better processes. The other benefit to this early simulation is that nontechnical business analysts quickly build and document test cases. This will cut testing and test maintenance time.

In the scenario step, three business rules for the decisions in the scenarios are gathered from the SMEs. Business rules might be expressed in business conversation form or directly in a formal form. In either case, formal vocabulary is gathered for the business rules.

A scenario model would not normally deal with fault handling on a technical level. However, business errors should be handled in the scenario. You might find a condition that triggers a rollback, meaning that we need to undo some steps and retry. Or, there might be an escalation of tasks that have gone past their due date. Again, we are not dealing with a system failure at this level. This type of error handling involves only business decisions.

In scenario modeling, process analysts conduct document modeling. They gather the types, attributes, and cardinalities of the documents. For instance, if our contract processes identified a receipt document, then the attributes of the receipts are completed. A receipt might have an item SCU, a shipping date, a receiving attribute, and other attributes.

Prior to scenario diagramming, IT staff might not be involved. Core and phase diagrams involve business logic and sequencing activities for appropriate resources. Scenario diagrams, however, may interface with IT assets such as databases, web services, and applications. Collaborating with IT architects while scenario modeling might result in a better understanding of expectations. By collaborating on scenarios, the IT staff may better prepare resources and assets for executing fully automated processes.

Step Four: Integration Modeling

As shown in Figure 1–7, process analysts add integration details to the scenario phase models. Integration details might include workflow patterns, which create a higher level of process coordination. SMEs identify data test cases for processes and decisions.

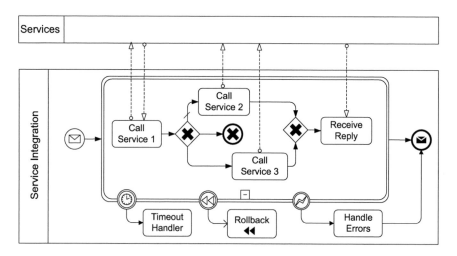

Figure 1–7   *Integration modeling diagrams add the necessary technical details.*

In integration modeling, business rules are positioned for use by decisions in processes. Business rules should be tested in the business rule system.

With a combination of process models and business rules, the integration modeling team sets up integrations with systems both internal and external to the firm. Integration modeling adds the logic that

- Orchestrates services.
- Standardizes or "wraps" services to provide a stable unchanging interface between scenarios and system integrations, called a *canonical*.
- Performs transformation/translation between scenario data and system data.

Business documents modeled in scenarios (leave requests, inventory replenishment, requisitions, etc.) are added to the flows of the process. Process analysts map the types and attributes. In integration modeling, process analysts might create more data types and documents that allow integration and error reporting. If there are multiple systems that perform a similar function, they create standard "business objects." For instance, if our government contract process interfaces with three receipting systems, then they build a single receipt business object.

Integration might also start the use of workflow patterns to coordinate the work of many process scenarios. For instance, in the government contracting example we will need to coordinate the approval of change orders and budgets.

More detail is added to process data models. There might be constraints on the XML schema. Business rules might need detailed enterprise data analysis in SQL. Business rules might need data services from databases in the environment.

Integration diagramming provides an opportunity to efficiently manage and reuse existing data and services. Often a new business object might be a hybrid of existing data. For example, you might want to use customer data and combine with order data for a "customer sales" data type. Both data types might already exist as services. Combining these two services eliminates the need to create and manage a new service. Traditional development methods might require a new service to be created for handling this hybrid object. As services evolve, changes must be made to the processes that use them. An integration process enables the IT staff to improve services without a major effect on existing scenarios.

Step Five: Services Modeling

In Step 5, the PMF merges processes into the SOA. Service modeling creates independent services that can be combined to realize significant, enterprise-level business processes. As shown in Figure 1–8, the types of services include business processes, decision services, and systems services.

A service can be defined as a low-level activity that is used frequently among multiple processes. A service might involve a specific data type and storage location. It might perform a data manipulation or implement a business rule. The

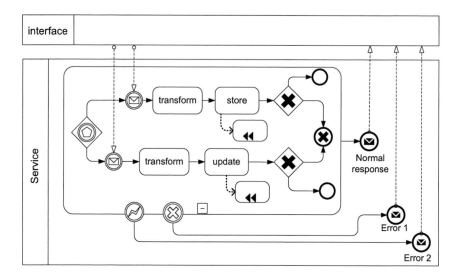

Figure 1–8   *The Services Modeling phase adds necessary fault handling details.*

operations should be generic, and not specific to any one business process. Services are often shared enterprise-wide.

In services modeling, the outputs of this step build important parts of the SOA. The activities of process modeling, business rules, and data modeling define

- Technical level communications.
- Orchestration or combining of services.
- Interoperability at a semantic level .

For each diagram in the scenario model, process and technical experts define detailed services. The services support a continuity of operation and survivability. A best practice for integrations is to create a set of common systems services. These systems services should

- Handle faults and errors.
- Handle transactions and rollback compensation.
- Transform trading partners' transaction data and our business process data types.

A complete business process acts on all the messages, including the system failures. In service modeling, BPMN diagrams have the necessary scheduling, exceptions, and compensations. The purpose of the details is to erect a more complete process model.

The process should handle every possible exception. There are three types of exceptions: business rules exceptions, technical exceptions, and system exceptions. The process should "compensate" for transactions that fail to complete. In compensation, the process cleans up or backs out records from ERPs. Prerequisite processes must complete and there could be "delay" actions noted on the diagram.

Business processes usually receive a message and translate it into another message that the next part of the process can understand. With BPMN, you can add advanced abilities, known as workflow patterns, that suspend processing or communicate with disconnected, mobile processes. Adding workflow patterns yields opportunities to fine-tune your most complicated practices.

The IT staff should be responsible for creating and maintaining services diagrams. The IT staff may often prefer to write code rather than create a diagram, but the code does not facilitate good communication with the business managers and SMEs. You might use UML or other technical diagrams for services. The business side of an organization often needs to know the inner workings of services, but either no diagram exists or the diagrams are too technical. If no diagram exists, the organization might require reverse engineering of business logic by reading code. If the diagrams are too technical, IT engineers might be needed to interpret them into a business language. Critical errors might be introduced in the reverse engineering effort due to inaccurate translation. Therefore, BPMN is a much better choice for services diagrams.

Other Considerations in Production

If legacy systems are involved in the projects, then management directs analysts and developers to perform convergences and refactoring techniques. On completion of application development, the analysts and developers position the systems in the IT infrastructure with process convergence. On completion of process convergence, processes and decisions are "instrumented" using Business Activity Monitoring (BAM).

As the model progresses, capabilities move from documentation through simulation and into execution. The business processes and business rules create user interfaces, Business-to-Business (B2B) integration, Commercial Off-The-Shelf (COTS) integration, and data warehouse ingredients. The metadata that describe these become important artifacts of the PMF approach.

SUMMARY

The overarching objective of process-modeling BPMN is to understand, institutionalize, improve, and control all the components of a business model. BPMN diagrams accurately and rapidly gather processes and business rules, digitized or otherwise. Without a formal approach, your firm probably gathers rules through legacy, paper-oriented procedures, or a loose tale of data models and use cases. Benefits of the SOA cannot be achieved this way.

We described the PMF. The core motivation of the PMF is to gather application requirements from the correct role with the correct method. The outcome is that lower-cost efforts create the process and decisions and then get them right.

CHAPTER 2

BPMN: BASICS AND GATEWAYS

THE BASIC SHAPES

In the introduction, we defined BPMN concepts as key parts of a business process model. This chapter presents BPMN shapes with the aim of matching the needs of a business process with the proper sequence of shapes.

Each BPMN symbol is classified by one of four shape types: rectangle, circle, line, or diamond. The shapes define classes of behaviors. Basic behaviors of the shape types include activities, gateways, events, sequences, and flows. Behavior is defined for each of these shape types by 'Markers' or shapes within. All shapes reside in a participant's pool. Also, shapes sequence with interactions or communicate with messages. With a grasp of the basic shapes and the markers, you can easily read BPMN diagrams. Before delving into detailed BPMN, we define the shape types.

Activities

An activity shape is represented by a rounded box, as exhibited here.

It defines where a process step occurs. Activity shapes include three basic types (see Table 2–1).

Table 2–1   Basic Types of Activity Shapes

Task
A rounded rectangle showing the finest or atomic
process step. It cannot be broken down to a finer level.

Subprocess (collapsed)
A rounded rectangle that can contain a series of other
steps. The other steps are hidden from view; the plus
sign indicates additional information.

+

Subprocess (expanded)
A rounded rectangle showing all the subprocess
activities (from the collapsed subprocess)

-

Looping Activity

An activity that repeats for multiple iterations is called a looping activity. Looping
activities can be either a task or a subprocess. The marker for the looping task or
subprocess is a pointed arc.

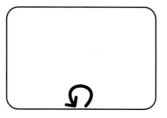

Looping Task

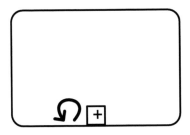

Looping Subprocess

The looping task is a simple activity, performed repeatedly; for instance, a wheel turns. Most often looping activities are subprocesses. Because it is a compound, multi-step activity, a looping subprocess can model a manufacturing assembly line. When the loop ends, the activity is complete, and the process continues to the next activity.

The loop is dependent on a condition—for example, "Tally votes while the polls are open." A text annotation might be used to specify the loop stopping condition.

Another looping activity type is the multiple instance subprocess. It completes in a predetermined number of iterations. The marker for the multiple instance subprocess is a series of three vertical lines.

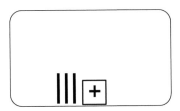

Multiple Instance Subprocess

The condition for the multiple instance subprocess might be a fixed number such as "5," or it might be assigned from the instance's process data—for example, "For each ordered item, add the item's price to the total." The multiple instance subprocess is not an ordinary looping subprocess. Use the loop symbol when the number of iterations is not known outside the activity. Use the multiple instance markers when the number of iterations is calculated externally.

Gateways

Gateways are represented by diamond shapes, as exhibited here.

The gateway shape either splits or merges transition flows in a process diagram. The diamond can be empty or have symbols. All gateways share a similar function—they divert a process into different flow paths. There are data, event, and parallel gateways. These are represented by different symbols. We cover gateway markings later in this chapter.

Events

All events are circular, as in the empty start shape as exhibited here.

The event shape defines a point of interest within the progress of the process. It can be at the start of a process (start event), within a process flow (intermediate event), or the end of a process (end event). These are shown in Table 2–2.

As in gateway shapes, each category of events (start, intermediate, and end) can be detailed with more shapes inside the circles. These express more process implementation details. Overall, the idea of a process event arises from an understanding of the basic circle shapes.

Participant Pool

The pool shape contains the elements of a process flow performed by the process participant. The pool shape is sometimes called a *swimlane*. The terms *lane* and *swimlane* can be ambiguous. Be careful not to confuse the term *swimlane* with a *BPMN lane*.

Table 2–2   Major Catagories of Event Shapes

Start event This is used at the start of a process. Start event shapes are drawn as a <u>single thin line</u> circle.	
Intermediate event This is used between the start and the end of a process. Start event shapes are drawn as a <u>double thin line</u> circle.	
End event This is used to show where a process flow may end. The shape is drawn with a **<u>thick solid line.</u>**	

The pool shape represents a participant. As stated in the introduction, a participant is anything involved in the process—a person, a system, or even another process.

Lane

As shown in Figure 2–1, a lane in BPMN is a subdivision of a pool. It graphically separates areas of the process diagram for more visibility and understanding.

A lane does not imply another process participant.[1] The lane shape in BPMN is a partition of the pool shape. Your diagram might use one pool and a separate lane to document activities for each participant. Yet, this may be an inaccurate model of your process. The proper usage of the lane shape classifies and organizes activities within a pool, according to the activities the pool is illustrating. A pool is used to show a single role, but when the role breaks down into overlapping subroles, lanes can be used to visually represent those subroles. For example, a group of clerks might perform the same job function, but some may have specialty skills. The specialty clerks might also do general work as well. In this case, there is no definite separation of the types of clerks. A lane within a pool might be used to separate the work performed only by specialty clerks from the general activities of all clerks.

---

1. A BPMN lane is not a *swimlane* from the unified modeling language term (UML) specification. Pool and Lane shapes are similar to the swimlane.

Figure 2–1   *A participant pool with lanes.*

Connecting Shapes: Sequences and Messages

BPMN shapes are connected with sequences and messages.

Sequence Flow Lines

A solid line with an arrowhead on one end represents sequence lines. The arrow shows process *sequence flow* direction.

   Sequence lines define the sequence flow, or transition, between the logical steps performed by a single participant. For instance, the contract is awarded after the bids are evaluated. "Bid Evaluation" transitions to "Contract Award" within the pool contract office.

   The concept of transition is represented by a sequence flow line. A sequence flow from one activity or event to the next shows the next as starting—or enabled to start. In the example, Bid Evaluation is complete and Contract Award is started. A pool involves one participant. You can only use sequence flow lines to transition activities to and from a pool.

Message Lines

Messages are represented with a dashed line, with a circle at the starting end and an arrowhead on the other end. The arrow shows the *message flow* direction.

The concept of interaction is represented by the message line. Participants interact with each other between pools using a message line. For instance, the "Contracting Officer" awards the winning bid to the "Contractor." The message is in the award. By definition, participants use messages to interact. Therefore, messages are always used between participant pools.

Miscellaneous

There are a number of miscellaneous BPMN shapes used for documentation purposes.

Diagram Artifacts

There are also diagram artifacts—text annotation, data objects, and groups. Artifacts are often associated with other shapes but do not have a sequence flow or message flow. The dotted association line is used to attach text and data artifacts to other BPMN shapes. Association lines attached to a data object may have an open arrowhead which indicates data going into or coming out of an activity. Be careful not to confuse the dotted association line with the dashed message line.

Text annotations are particularly useful, as they can provide more detail about an activity than can normally fit into a label.

```
Text Annotation with more
details about an activity
```

Activities, events, and gateways will normally have a short label. One goal of creating a BPMN diagram should be to minimize the risk of misinterpretation through better descriptions. A good BPMN diagram, however, should also be concise. Not all readers of a diagram will be BPMN experts. By using text annotations, a broader audience can be reached while still using well-formed BPMN labels.

The data object is a rectangle with the upper right corner folded over, as shown here.

Purchase Order

The text label for a data object can be found underneath the shape. You may often find the current state of the data object as an attribute shown in brackets under the text label. As the diagram progresses, the state of the data object can easily be read, as displayed in Figure 2–2.

As with the text annotation, the association line attaches the data object to another shape. As an artifact, data objects often are associated with flow objects, but may also be associated with tasks, gateways, events, sequence lines, or message lines. In message flow, data objects portray the "payload" or content of messages.

The use of data objects is optional. Some diagrams may concentrate on flow, while others show the complete details. Data objects provide more information without changing the basic behavior of the process. In a Pi-Calculus processing model, data is not passed from task to task. Process data resides in a common pool shared by all activities. Associating data objects with sequence flow might show that the artifact is required before the process can transition to the next activity. Data artifacts do not directly affect the sequence or message flows. You might find a data object associated with an activity, which signifies where the data is produced. Associating data objects with a gateway can show the data on which a decision is based.

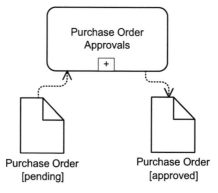

Figure 2–2   *Use of data object shapes.*

Data modeling is just as critical as process and decision modeling. A data object is a visual depiction of the modeled subject or "business entity." A data model may depict an electronic form or a physical document. Data objects provide information about what activities need to be performed and/or what they produce. For instance, an inventory manager might requisition special items. The "requisition" would be a data item.

Groups

The group shape defines a common purpose to a group of shapes. The group shape is drawn as a rounded corner rectangle with a dot-dash-dot-dash pattern, as shown here.

The group shape is permitted on the process diagram layer above pools and lanes. A group shape surrounds other shapes located anywhere in the diagram. A group illustrates related activities, even when they cross multiple participants (see Figure 2–3). As an alternative to a subprocess, the group shape might surround shapes inside the pool. The difference between a group and a subprocess is that a group does not have a process flow associated with it.

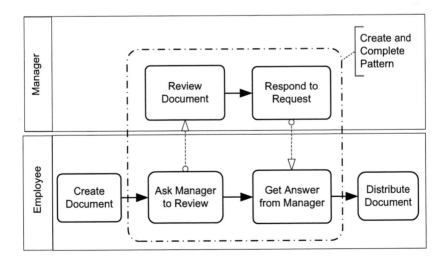

Figure 2–3 *The group shape encircles related activities in two participant pools.*

USING THE BASIC SHAPES:
PUTTING IT ALL TOGETHER

With our understanding of these basic shapes, let's start building a diagram. We will use examples from the introduction's process archetypes.

Suppose we are developing core business processes for a contract administration system. In BPMN, a part of the basic flow of activities is shown as that depicted in Figure 2–4. A parallel split flow might also appear, as shown in Figure 2–5.

In parallel branches, process flow might progress through any number of activities. Your understanding of the process decides parallel activity. You might observe activities and dependencies in your organization. Branches might merge, or other branches might complete while other activities might continue to progress through the process.

Implicit Merge

In a simple merge, the flow paths are rejoined. Consider an item in an inventory process that moves through an inspection process. If there is no defect, it is noted that the next activity is "Mark Passed." Otherwise, the defect is identified and reported. In Figure 2–6, the paths that split after "Inspect" are rejoined (merged) at "Shelf Item. "

This is called an implicit merge because the merge is implied—the tasks merge with undefined conditions. The diagram fragment in Figure 2–6 does not specify *how* the Mark Passed task and "Report Defect" merge. The diagram's intentions might initially seem clear; however, the design approach is deceiving. Implicit merges are ambiguous. Since it is implicit, we cannot precisely detect what happens at the merge point on Shelf Item. Here the process might continue uninterrupted from Mark Passed to Shelf Item. Otherwise, the process might wait until both Mark Passed and Report Defect tasks complete before continuing to Shelf Item. Because there is no flow control, the Shelf Item task might execute more than once. We suggest you define only one transition from Inspect to avoid implicit process merges. Otherwise, the process diagram should describe the merge behavior at the Shelf Item point with more shapes.

Figure 2–7 shows a choice in defining conditions for the two paths leaving the Inspect Item task.

The diamond symbol on a transition path shows the process path when data matches a specified transition condition. The sequence flow line with the slash marks a default path. A "condition" is a Boolean expression, based on process data that controls a sequence of activities. For instance, a condition might examine the value of a "Pass Inspection" flag and follow the transition to Mark Passed when the value is "YES." We say the condition *evaluates* whether or not it is true. The process follows this path when the transition condition fails to be true. You should always use a default path whenever conditional paths are specified.

Figure 2–4   *Sequence flow.*

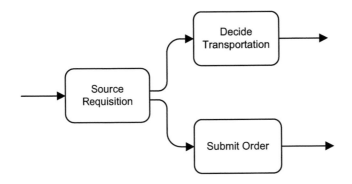

Figure 2–5   *Simple parallel split.*

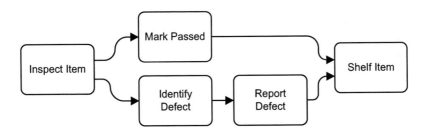

Figure 2–6   *Implicit merge in an inventory process.*

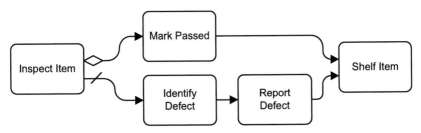

Figure 2–7   *Splitting paths with a condition.*

Figure 2–7 shows how the process takes a path to either Mark Passed or "Identify Defect." A default path clearly states that either path can occur, but not both. By definition, the default path has no condition. The default path indicates the sequence flow that is taken when all other paths do not meet their proscribed conditions.

BPMN SHAPE USAGE

Gateways

A gateway splits or merges paths in a BPMN diagram at a specific point. Gateways direct sequence flows with data, or they specify various path splits. When used as a merge point, a gateway clarifies the implicit merge.

The simple gateway shape is an empty diamond, as shown here.

The simple gateway shape does not specify a behavior. In the BPMN specification, there is no difference between the empty gateway shape and the data-based exclusive gateway. Because the data-based exclusive gateway has an explicit behavior, we recommend using it instead. A process diagram in Figure 2–8 shows the exclusive gateway with an X inside the diamond. For the rest of this book, we will favor the use of more descriptive gateway shapes.

Data-based Exclusive Gateways

The data-based exclusive gateway is a diamond shape with an enclosed X, as shown here.

The data-based gateway shapes are called either *exclusive* or *inclusive*. In the data-based "exclusive" gateway, process data defines conditions for the paths

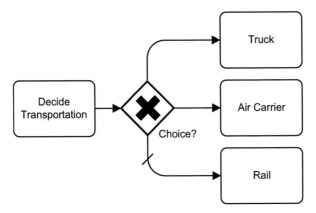

Figure 2–8 *Data-based exclusive gateway.*

leaving the gateway. The gateway is also called exclusive when the process moves along only one path, excluding all other paths. For example, examine Figure 2–8.

Returning to our process archetypes, Truck, Air Carrier, and Rail tasks appear after deciding what form of transportation will be used. The gateway specifies exclusive behavior, the flow takes only one path, and all others are excluded. The sequence flow line to the Rail task has a marker indicating the default path. The choice of the Rail Transportation as the default is a design choice. Again, always use a default path whenever conditional flows exist.

Parallel Gateways

A parallel gateway is a diamond shape with an enclosed cross, as shown here.

In the parallel gateway, all paths leaving the gateway are executed (see Figure 2–9). This gateway is used in a part of the process that needs to follow all branches. All the activities occur simultaneously. This is best when it is not efficient for sequential execution. One long-running activity might delay everything else in the process. For this, we use the parallel gateway shape to show multiple activities being performed simultaneously.

There is no default condition when a parallel gateway is used. All paths are always taken and the transition to all paths occurs at the same time.

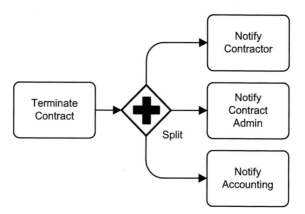

Figure 2–9   *Parallel gateway—all paths will be taken simultaneously.*

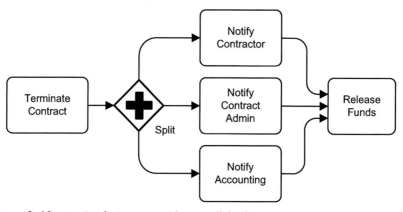

Figure 2–10   *An implicit merge with a parallel split.*

When deciding whether or not to use a parallel gateway, there are several things to consider:

- Are all tasks always executed? If not, use a data-based gateway.
- Are there any tasks in the sequence that depend on each other? When there is a dependency, use a sequence of tasks.
- What is the impact on the resulting tasks if all paths occur simultaneously?
- In later activities, should the process continue sequentially rather than in parallel? This determines where the parallel sequence flows need to merge before subsequent tasks can begin.

Explicit Gateway Merge

An explicit merge uses a gateway shape to specify multiple paths merging. Figure 2–10 shows implicitly merging paths after a gateway shape.

Exactly what happens at the merge point—the "Release Funds" task? The parallel gateway following the "Terminate Contract" task says that notification of the contractor, contract administrator, and accounting occurs in parallel. Each begins at the same time. The notification tasks take different times to complete. One may finish before the others. The diagram does not define what happens at the merge point. Potentially, the Release Funds task could occur three times. Here is an example of why:

> After the Terminate Contract task, the three notification tasks begin. Suppose Notify Accounting completes before Notify Contract Administration and transitions to the Release Funds task, then continues through the following steps. Meanwhile, the activity at the Notify Contract Admin task completes a few hours later. Next, a new copy of the Release Funds task begins. It continues processing the flow. Finally, the Notify Contractor completes, and so forth. Consequently, the Release Funds activity has occurred three times. If this is the intent of the process, then the design in Figure 2–10 is correct.

Implicit merges are usually ambiguous and confusing. Figure 2–11 depicts this possible scenario. It also shows what could occur in each path.

If the Release Funds task should not occur three times, then the process might be clearer with a parallel merge. The parallel merge shape is identical to the parallel split. Placement is the only difference between the parallel split and merge.

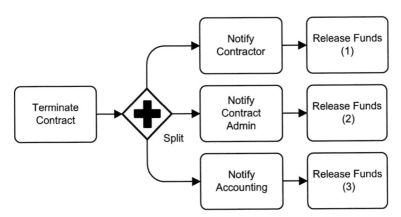

Figure 2–11   *Illustrating the ambiguity of the implicit merge.*

At the diagram's merge point, before the Release Funds task, all paths must complete before continuing. The Release Funds task is dependent on the three notifications completing; the process will coordinate all paths.

In contrast to a parallel merge shape, the exclusive gateway merges paths, but with different behavior. Figure 2–13 depicts a fragment of a supply chain process.

The data-based exclusive shape can merge (here, three notifying activities). The gateway use is optional for exclusive paths. Because one path emerges from the gateway after the "Terminate Transport" task, you might connect the lines from the notification tasks directly to the "Reverse Freight" task. The exclusive data path specifies the merge point, or the latter Reverse Freight task is run.

Use of the exclusive gateway shape for a merge point is good standard practice. For diagram clarity, we recommend using an explicit merge point. In Figure 2–13, the exclusive gateways for both split and merge document the end of the three paths. As a diagram becomes more detailed, dozens of steps might happen between Terminate Transport and Reverse Freight. Again, the behavior of the implicit merge can be confusing. This might be especially true if a process diagram spans many pages. Consider viewing large diagrams on computer screens, scrolling back and forth to see the entire flow. If you explicitly use merge shapes, the diagram becomes much easier to read. Because parallel and inclusive gateway shapes need a shape to merge flows, the exclusive merge gateway shape is consistent with the rest of the diagram.

Data-Based Inclusive Gateway

The data-based inclusive gateway is a diamond shape with an enclosed circle, as shown here.

It is called inclusive because multiple paths could be taken. The gateway evaluates process data against a condition, which is where the term "data-based" comes from. The gateway includes all sequence flows that have a condition that evaluates to "True."

The inclusive gateway shape is a hybrid of the data-based exclusive and parallel gateways. There is a condition for each flow path. One or more of the conditional paths might be taken.

Figure 2–14 presents a fragment of an order management process. Depending on the order total, various processing steps must be taken.

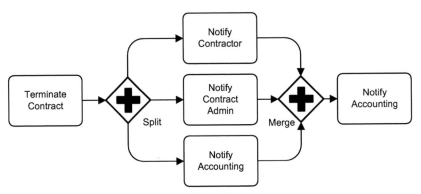

Figure 2–12 *Proper merging of parallel paths.*

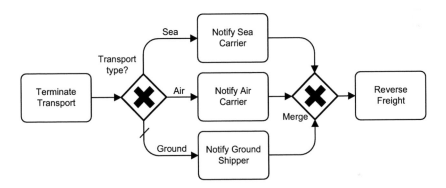

Figure 2–13 *An explicit merge for the exclusive data-based gateway, with a default condition.*

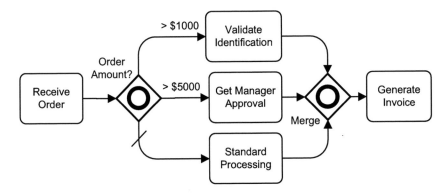

Figure 2–14 *An explicit merge with a data-based inclusive gateway.*

After the Receive Order task, the other paths execute whenever associated conditions are true. If the order amount is over $1000, extra validation occurs to prevent fraud. Additionally, orders over $5000 must be approved by a manager. When none of the conditional paths are taken, the process takes the default path. If the order total is not over $1000, only the standard processing activity occurs.

As with parallel gateways, care should be taken when merging inclusive paths. Consider the process flow after the Standard Processing task, if we specify no default path. If no default path is specified, and no condition evaluates to True, a deadlock occurs. In a deadlock, the process cannot go past the gateway. It never continues or stops. If your process needs inclusive gateways, then verify that each gateway has a default path.

As with other gateways, the BPMN specification allows implicit merging for data-based gateways. Again, your design should be clear at the point where sequence flows merge. The use of explicit merging for parallel and implicit gateway shapes is a good best practice.

Sometimes a process might perform an added activity under certain conditions. It might bypass activities under other conditions. An activity is not compulsory on every branch coming from a gateway.

In Figure 2–15, the Receive Order process takes the extra step ("Get Manager Approval") when the order amount is more than $5000. By default, the Get Manager Approval activity is bypassed. It is simple to create a default path to bypass the extra step.

Inclusive gateways might also use transitions without activities. In Figure 2–16, the process's default path bypasses all the conditional paths. Without one or more conditions in the gateway evaluating to True, the process takes the default path—straight to the merge point—lacking activities.

Figure 2–16 shows an order management process fragment. The "Standard Processing" task in Figure 2–15 was replaced with a default path void of activity. As an inclusive gateway, the default path is not taken if any conditional path is True. One or more other tasks ("Validate Identification," "Manager Approval") can occur in parallel.

Gateway Labels

The gateway lines in Figures 2–13 through 2–16 are labeled. You might document gateway conditions with labels in question form. For instance, "Selected color?" would be a good label. The sequence flow lines transitioning from the gateway should be labeled to answer the question the gateway asks. The answers "red," "blue," and "green" could be possible answers to the question.

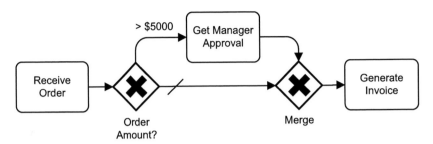

Figure 2–15   *A data-based exclusive gateway controlling an optional step.*

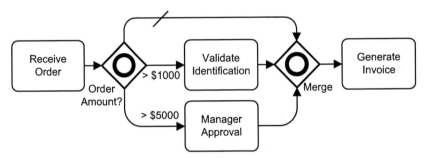

Figure 2–16   *Inclusive gateway with a default bypass path.*

Inclusive / Exclusive Gateway Best Practices

There are a few best practices that should be considered:

- Limit use of the inclusive gateway. Instead, try to use multiple exclusive gateways.
- Avoid using the inclusive gateway where the conditions are not related, such as document gateways. A gateway comment should ask only one question or state only one condition. For example, "Selected color?", "Low inventory," and "Order amount more than $5000" can be assigned to separate exclusive gateways.

Using a Subprocess for Complex Merge

There is a shape for complex merges, called Complex Merge Gateway. The complex gateway is a diamond shape with an enclosed asterisk, as shown here.

Because subprocesses have an implicit parallel split and merge, the subprocess can solve complex merge challenges. We recommend avoiding using the complex split and merge. Instead, the subprocess can achieve the same diagram goal.

The patterns in Figures 2–17 and 2–18 are equivalent. Figure 2–18 is more compact and uses a subprocess implicit split and merge pattern. There is probably justification for using a subprocess in Figure 2–17, even without the complex merge. To improve clarity in Figure 2–18, you might use a parallel gateway before the Truck Transport and Material Safety tasks, and leave the rest unchanged. Either way, it means the same. It can be simple to see the implicit split and merge patterns in the subprocesses. Outside a subprocess, use explicit splits and merges.

When choosing a pattern, ask the question, "Will adding the explicit split or merge add clarity to my diagram or will it add clutter?"

The complex merge gateway shown in Figure 2–19 is used for the same pattern in Figures 2–17 and 2–18. We do not recommend using this shape. All the logic from a complex merge shape can be defined in a subprocess (Figure 2–18). If you do not wish to use the subprocess, use explicit merges (Figure 2–17). Using the complex merge shape might require the reader to backtrack.

Ad-hoc Subprocess

Ad-hoc activities must be completed, yet the order in which they are performed is unknown. The ad-hoc subprocess performs activities in an unspecified order.

Figure 2–20 depicts a vendor evaluation process from the introduction's Supplier Relations Management (SRM) archetype. The four activities must be completed, yet there is no apparent order to the evaluation steps.

Activities inside any subprocess start with the first shape in a sequence flow. When sequence flow is not defined, all the subprocess activities start simultaneously. All activities must end before the subprocess is complete. Therefore, subprocesses also include an implicit merge.

An ad-hoc subprocess shows activities that will likely be performed in a sequence, but whose order is not defined. A tilde marker is shown on the subprocess

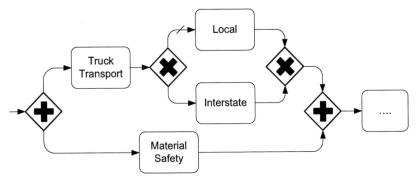

Figure 2–17   *A complex merge pattern with explicit merge.*

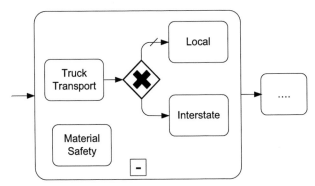

Figure 2–18   *A complex merge pattern using a subprocess.*

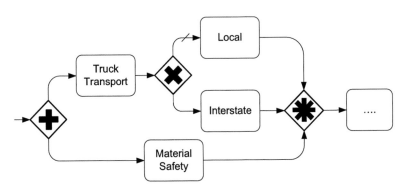

Figure 2–19   *The complex merge gateway.*

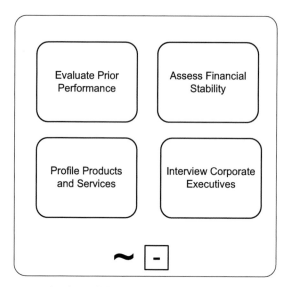

Figure 2–20   *Example of an ad-hoc process.*

shape when it is ad-hoc. The ad-hoc behavior is different than an implicit split in a subprocess. For example, a grocery list could be shown as an ad-hoc subprocess. All items on the list are required, but items are added to the cart as they are found in the store—in no specific order. In a parallel pattern, all items would be simultaneously added to a cart. The subprocess without the ad-hoc marker shows the parallel pattern.

The ad-hoc subprocess simplifies some complex patterns. You might use the ad-hoc subprocess during the development of a diagram when the execution order is yet unknown. A parallel split or a defined sequence flow with gateways describes most processes. In our shopping cart example, however, the ad-hoc subprocess shows the desired pattern with the minimum number of shapes.

SUMMARY

There are three broad categories of BPMN shapes:

- A shape that holds the activities and events: the participant pool.
- Next there are the things within the pool: activities, gateways and events.
- Finally there are several miscellaneous shapes used for documentation.

In the introduction, we defined a business process as *a flow of decision-coordinated activities, conducted by participants and acting on data, information, and knowledge that reach a goal.*

We covered the shapes for activities (rounded rectangles), participants (rectangles), gateways (diamond), interactions and messages (lines) and miscellaneous shapes.

We have broken our description of BPMN into two chapters: one on basics and gateways, and one on events. In our training material we have discovered this order promotes good understanding of the BPMN approach to process modeling.

CHAPTER 3

BPMN: EVENTS AND SUMMARY

EVENTS

In the introduction, we defined BPMN concepts as key parts of a business process model. This chapter presents BPMN event shapes with the idea of matching the needs of a business process with the proper sequence of shapes.

To grasp the concepts in this chapter, you should understand the material in the previous chapter on BPMN basics and gateways. An understanding of explicit and implicit merges is also important.

In the diagrams from the last chapter, our process began with a task shape. The BPMN specification allows a process to start with either a task or a gateway. A start event, however, is often a better choice for starting a process diagram. Start events explicitly show how and where the process starts. Let's begin our discussion of events with the empty start and events shapes (see Figure 3–1).

Consider this diagram without the start and end events. With or without the start and end events, the process in the diagram says the same thing. The events clarify the start and end points for the reader.

There can only be one start event. The end event, however, may be used more than once in a pool. Figure 3–2 shows the usage of more than one end event.

Adding the gateway after the "First Step" task, the optional path is the "Optional Step" task. Under certain conditions, the process simply ends. A process end is an event, not a task. Therefore, the empty end event shape is more fit-

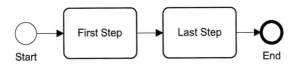

Figure 3–1   *Start and end event example.*

51

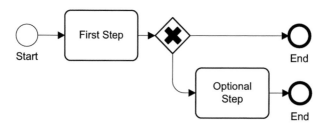

Figure 3–2   *Ending example with a gateway.*

ting for this scenario. Adding the end event simplifies the diagram. Without the end event after the Optional Step task, there would be an implicit end. Explicit shapes improve a process design's clarity.

The intermediate empty shape, the double circle, specifies an interesting point in the diagram or shows a point where the state or status changes. Because the shape is an empty event and behavior is not specified, the description for this shape is vague. Consider a business process that has entered a new status. For example, it might transition from a "pending" status to "approved."

The intermediate empty event documents a point, such as a Key Performance Indicator (KPI), in the diagram. KPIs are metrics used to quantify objectives that reflect the strategic performance of an organization. When a status changes to "rejected" in the process example, a KPI might be the number of rejected requests. In addition to status counts, the process might record more process data at this point. To track these, businesses build business intelligence (BI) and business activity monitoring (BAM) into their processes. KPIs are an example of the use of the intermediate empty event (IEE) (see Figure 3–3).

The rules for the proper use of the intermediate empty event include the following:

1. A transition line must leave and enter an intermediate shape; otherwise an IEE should be a start or end event.

2. The IEE shape never receives a message from another participant. That is, a message (dashed) line should not enter or leave the intermediate empty event.

3. The IEE does not show any delay in the process.

4. The IEE does not have any conditions associated with it.

5. The IEE does not imply a point of synchronization.

So, the empty event shape's usefulness is limited. Now we will take a look at interesting event shapes that specify certain conditions and behaviors.

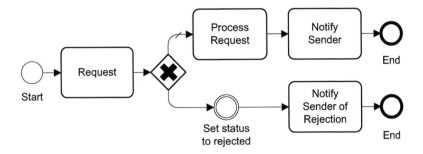

Figure 3–3 *Examples of an intermediate event.*

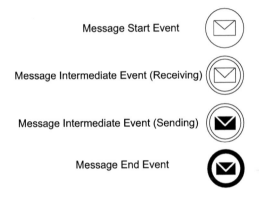

Figure 3–4 *The four BPMN message events.*

Message Event

There are three types of message events—start, intermediate, and end. Like the empty start, intermediate, and end shapes, the thin line, double line, and thick line mark where they can be used within a process flow.

The message shapes display an envelope icon in the center. Each inherits the rules of the respective empty start, intermediate, and end event shapes (see Figure 3–4). The start shape event is used at the beginning of a process diagram, and has no sequence flow lines entering it. The end event shape cannot have any sequence flow leaving it. The rules are reversed for interactions or message flows. Message start events always receive a message with the line arrowhead pointing at the shape. Message end events can only send messages, with the arrowhead of the message line pointing away from the shape.

Figure 3–5 shows the use of each message event shape. The BPMN specification allows the intermediate message event to show message lines entering and

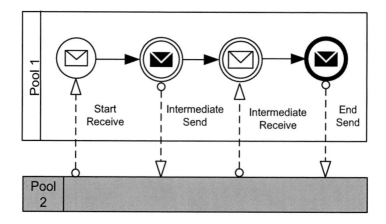

Figure 3–5   *Examples of the four types of messages.*

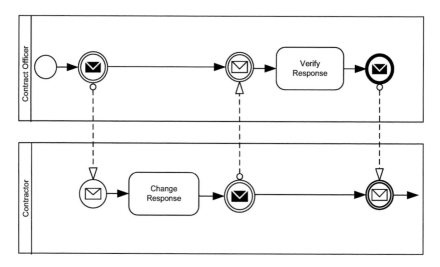

Figure 3–6   *Use of message events between participants. The process is complete when the message in the top pool is sent.*

leaving the shape. However, the intermediate message cannot simultaneously send and receive. Pools represent participants, and a message is between two participants. Therefore, a message communicates between participants. Messages never occur from one shape to another within the same pool. Messages (dashes with open arrows) only occur between pools.

So far, we have covered enough shapes to start building an accurate process model. Figure 3–6 shows two pools, representing two participants. There is a mixture of empty events and message events. First, the empty start event shape in the pool labeled "Contract Officer" shows the start of the process. From the perspective of the "Contractor," the process starts when a message is received from the Contract Officer. Before this event, the Contractor is not involved in this process.

The message start event will not start until a message triggers the event. Then it transitions to the next step ("Change Response") in the process. The message might be a simple trigger signal that starts the process, or it may contain process data.

Tasks can be portrayed as start, intermediate, or end shapes. Tasks also can send or receive messages. As with the intermediate message event, a task cannot simultaneously send and receive a message. Sending and receiving a message needs two tasks or two intermediate message events.

So, if a task and an intermediate message event are nearly interchangeable, which one should you use? As a guideline, if a participant creates a message while working, it should be a task sending a message. Otherwise, a process responds to an external event, and the process models the message as an intermediate message event.

Consider an active office environment. A person completes a certain activity and passes a message to someone in another department to perform a step of the business process. To finish the process, this person awaits receipt of information from the other department. However, while waiting for the needed information, this person is busy with other tasks. The business process continues when the information arrives. Using a task to represent a participant awaiting information is allowed in the BPMN specification. However, this implies that the participant has only one job—to wait. In a system-to-system process, this may be an accurate statement, but in a person-to-person process, this is unlikely.

From the perspective of the participant represented by each pool, the intermediate message events connote the waiting of a process instance until receipts of messages are received from the other participant. The ending for the Contract Officer participant in Figure 3–6 is an ending message end event. There are important rules for dealing with message events:

- A start message event will never send a message; it only receives.
- An end message event will only send a message; it will never receive.
- An intermediate message event can either send or receive a message, but not both simultaneously.
- When a message is being received in an intermediate event, use the empty envelope (white). When a message is being sent, use the filled envelope (black).
- It is possible to have a message line coming in and going out of an intermediate message event, but only for bidirectional messaging. Bidirectional messages send an acknowledgement response from the

receiving participant as part of a single interaction. You may encounter
this pattern in technical diagrams. Bidirectional messaging is always
drawn in pairs. The line on the left side represents the message initiator.
The line on the right represents the acknowledgement response.

A business process has one starting point. Processes might start multiple
ways, but there is one starting point from the perspective of each participant. For
example, a process participant might start process activity by receiving an email, a
fax, or a phone call. Regardless of how participants receive information, they
finish their work the same way after receipt of the starting message. Depending on
the data received, there might be multiple outcomes or multiple end events. Also,
the processes might wait for information from other participants to continue at
multiple intermediate message events. If the design requires two or more starting
points, then break the process into multiple processes. Otherwise, redraw the process with a single start event followed by a gateway that decides how to proceed. If
neither option portrays the process accurately, then use the event-driven exclusive
gateway.

Event-Driven Exclusive Gateway

A process that receives multiple start messages with different data types calls for a
special symbol—the event-driven gateway with intermediate message events.

The event-driven exclusive gateway is a diamond shape with an intermediate
event shape inside (double thin line), as shown in Figure 3–7. The circle indicates
that this gateway type deals with events. Inside the circle there is a pentagon. The
pentagon in BPMN signifies multiple types of events. The Multiple Event symbol
in BPMN 1.0 was the six-sided star, which has since been changed to the pentagon.
You may still see the six-sided star shown in Figure 3–8 in some older diagrams.

The event-driven exclusive gateway awaits the first arriving message or event.
Events can include ordinary messages, signals, and timers. There is a specific pattern for this gateway. It might seem more intuitive that messages and events
should occur before the gateway, so the notation appears backwards. The event
shapes are drawn on the right side of the event-driven gateway or downstream.
Placing the events on the left (upstream) side would be a collection of events that
merge upon the gateway.

The event-driven exclusive gateway might appear in the middle of a process,
or it might be in a sequence as an intermediate shape. Figure 3–9 shows the use of
the event-driven gateway at the start of a process.

The event gateway is not a start event—neither are the following messages
and events. The gateway and its starting messages are intermediate types. The
gateway shape substitutes a start event—it awaits the activation of the downstream event shapes. Here, there is only one defined start point, but with this
gateway, processes can start multiple ways.

Figure 3–7   *Event-driven gateway symbol.*

Figure 3–8   *Event-driven gateway symbol (BPMN version 1.0).*

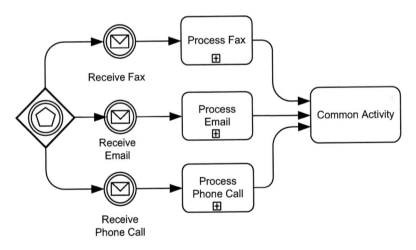

Figure 3–9   *Event-driven exclusive gateway used as a start event.*

When used as the start event, the event-based exclusive gateway indicates a new process instance for each event. In Figure 3–9, the receipt of a fax will cause one process instance. A subsequent receipt of an email on the gateway would spawn a different process instance, separate from the instance started by the fax message. If the process starts after multiple dependant messages or events, you should use a parallel gateway instead.

In Figure 3–9, three different event shapes start the activities. The example considers the email message event, which is partly human-based. The process also shows a "Receive Email" step. Once an intermediate message is received and the process instance starts, it merges back into either a people or systems process. The process needs initialization through one of many possible message types. Each message type requires different activity steps to process it. Alternately, you could draw the process with a single message start, followed by a gateway that determines the message type received. But the event gateway is a compact way of drawing this pattern and is more explicit.

The first activity in Figure 3–10, "Call External System," needs an answer from an external system. A message gateway awaits the system's response. The external system may be owned by another organization and controlled by their resources. In today's networked business world, this happens often. There are several reasons for separating the responses. A delay period occurs between sending and receiving the request. This is also an asynchronous interaction.

The external system responds with one of three different messages. Because the message format is different for each condition, three different message types receive the message. This pattern uses a single message event followed by an exclusive gateway. In many processes, however, the message types returned from other participants may differ and may require mappings to the needed message types. If the message type is not exactly the same, use different message shapes combined with an event-driven gateway.

This process pattern is useful when there are multiple suppliers or partner organizations. We will refer to these as external participants. Often, the external participant has varying degrees of system automation capabilities. Some external participants might support a Web services interaction, while others support file uploads. Still others need support for a manual process. Each method of receiving input needs different incoming message processing. Therefore, the event-driven exclusive gateway is a good choice for diagramming this pattern. We will discuss the patterns for the event-driven gateway in more detail in Chapter 5, "Patterns: BPMN for Combining Workflows."

Terminate Event

The Terminate event causes all activities in a process to be immediately ended, and its shape in a BPMN diagram is depicted as shown here.

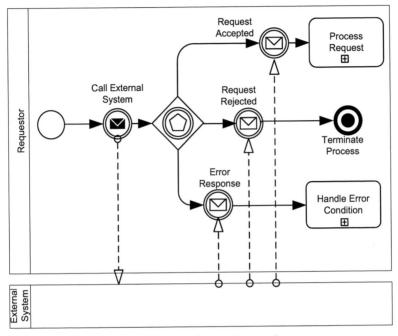

Figure 3–10 *Event-driven gateway used as an intermediate event.*

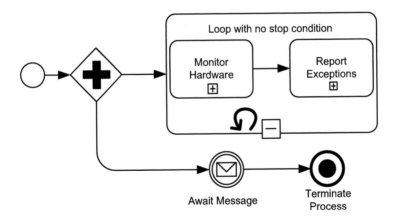

Figure 3–11 *A process with a conditional starting event.*

You can use the Terminate event shape to cancel all activities in a process. In Figure 3–11, the "Monitor Hardware" and "Report Exceptions" activities execute in a looping subprocess indefinitely. In parallel, a message event waits for a message before terminating the process.

If the Terminate message is received, then all the activities in the process are terminated.

A Terminate event causes all branches of a parallel sequence to stop. This is in contrast to the End event, which only stops one branch. Use an End event when the process is ending in a normal way. Use a Terminate event shape when you want to stop all activity in the pool immediately.

Timer Events

The Timer event is one of the more versatile shapes in BPMN. It expresses a time gap in processing or a wait for a period of time, or it triggers actions on tardy events, activities, or other processes. The Timer events include the start and intermediate, but there is no Timer end event. The start event (*left*) and intermediate event (*right*) appear as shown.

In Figure 3–12, the start Timer event shows that a process starts in a given time period. For example, the system runs a report on the last day of each month.

A specified time period could be a given day (such as every Friday), the last day of the month, or the first day of each quarter. You could also specify a time period such as two hours or three days.

The intermediate Timer event in Figure 3–13 expresses a process wait for a period of time before continuing. Like the Timer start shape, the time period may be expressed as a duration, or it may be a calendar date.

The intermediate Timer event expresses when something is not done within a certain time period; we want to take an alternate action such as an escalation path.

In subprocesses, the intermediate event catches a timeout condition. This is shown as a subprocess shape, with the intermediate event attached to the border of the subprocess. Any number of activities takes place in the subprocess. The alternate path starts in Figure 3–14 when the employee does not complete the work within the allotted time period.

The alternate flow transitioning from the Timeout event in Figure 3–14 is called an exception flow. Any intermediate event on a subprocess border produces an exception flow. Exception flow can be routed to a task or a subprocess. It is likely that more than one simple task will be required to handle an exception flow. As a best practice, we recommend using a subprocess activity to handle exception flow. If only one task is desired, use a collapsed subprocess.

Figure 3–12   *A time-driven report.*

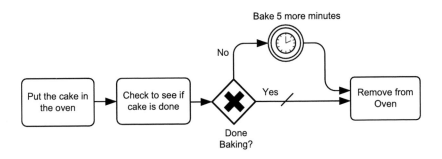

Figure 3–13   *A timer event used as an intermediate event.*

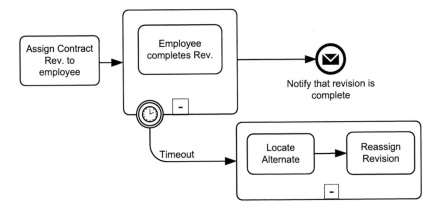

Figure 3–14   *Timer event used as an intermediate event.*

In this example, a manager submits a work request to an employee. When the employee finishes the work on schedule, a task completion message is sent to the manager. When the employee does not complete the task on schedule, however, the manager performs the steps in the escalation path. The intermediate event on the subprocess border simplifies the diagram. Consider the design that is required without attaching intermediate shapes to a border of a subprocess. This simple scenario may require multiple gateways, events, and complex merge patterns.

Figure 3–15 shows an intermediate Timer shape used within an event-driven gateway. In the example, a worker submits a request to a manager. The manager will either accept or reject the request. If the manager does not reply within a specified time period, the event-driven gateway is triggered and the process flow takes the respective gateway branch.

The details of the activities being performed by the manager are not displayed (the pool is collapsed). The message for each response type is different according to the timer, the acceptance, or the rejection.

The example in Figure 3–14 is similar to Figure 3–15; however, the event-driven gateway in Figure 3–15 ignores events on the other branches when they occur. In contrast, Figure 3–14 shows ongoing work and the manager is notified in parallel.

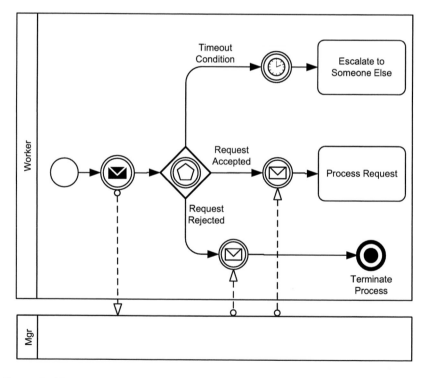

Figure 3–15   *Timer event used as an intermediate event.*

Normal sequence flow resumes after an exception flow sequence completes. Therefore, merging the exception flow with the normal flow is optional. If the normal sequence has stopped, the exception flow should merge with the normal flow. Other event shapes on the subprocess border might catch a condition when normal sequence flow ceases.

Throwing and Catching Events

Many event shapes might throw and catch an event. An event is thrown when the event condition is triggered by the shape. An event is caught by the shape designated to handle the thrown condition. In previous examples, message events are displayed with a filled icon sending and the message (and the unfilled icon) receiving.

The term *sending* might also mean *throwing*. The term *receiving* might mean *catching*. This same pattern exists with the other event shapes. Filled icons specify an event thrower (sends) and unfilled icons specify an event catcher (receives).

Error Events

The Error event shapes either cause an error flag to be raised, or catch and handle an error condition. When an error condition is raised, we call this a *throw*, meaning that the error throws the condition. The error condition is then caught by another shape. The Error event shapes include the intermediate Error event and the Error end event. Similar to the Message intermediate events, there are two variations of the Error intermediate event—the unfilled (white) icon for the catching version, and the filled (black) icon for the throwing version. There is no Error start event. The intermediate, throwing, catching, and ending error events are displayed left to right.

Process models often specify error conditions with a pair—a throwing end error and a catching intermediate error connected to a subprocess. End error events, not handled in the scope of the subprocess or larger process, do not need this matching intermediate process.

Like the Timer event, Error events can be connected to a subprocess or to a transition.

Errors arise from a number of conditions. Web services and databases might be offline for longer periods than a "service-level" required. Data from employees or trading partners might be incorrect. Errors can be detected in the process data through business rules or in combination with different events in the process. It is often necessary to define a number of errors for different conditions.

Error events throw variables that can be caught by subsequent intermediate errors. In a subprocess, you might need different error handling procedures for different conditions. Figure 3–16 shows one scenario.

Despite unpredictable circumstances, your processes must continue to run. Error shapes manage these unpredictable events. Errors work in pairs or sequences of throw and catch. In this subprocess, "Evaluate Data Conditions" might check for conditions in a database. When attributes in the process flow do not match an expected condition in Figure 3–16, the "Invalid Data" error is thrown. An intermediate error event catches the error and handles the issue. Because "Validate Data Conditions" uses database SQL, different irrecoverable errors might occur. For instance, a change in the schema or table structures might occur. The interface to the database should throw an error. In the example, these are caught by the intermediate "Other Errors" activity.

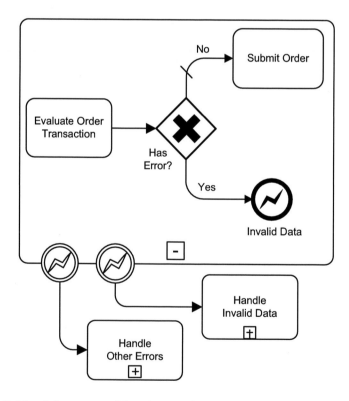

Figure 3–16   *Subprocesses with an intermediate error event.*

At mature enterprises, databases have Service-Level Agreements (SLAs). Databases should return query results within a certain time interval. As shown in Figure 3–17, we can easily add timers to the example to accommodate.

In this example, database middleware throws an error corresponding to a timeout. The error in this example would be caught by the Other Errors activity. The Timer event might be set to a period shorter than the middleware error. The Terminate end event would terminate all activities in the scope of the subprocess or process.

You should not design processes that create exceptions in parallel, especially when the exception flow merges with normal, post-subprocess flow. This could cause an unresolved, complex merge pattern. Here, each gateway type could create either a deadlock (two or more items, each awaiting the others to complete) or duplicate sequence flow. As mentioned, the subprocess can solve complex merge challenges. If the process calls for multiple error conditions in parallel,

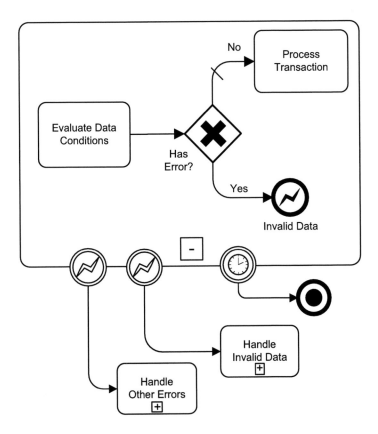

Figure 3–17   *Subprocesses with intermediate Error event and timer.*

it then places the subprocess, along with its error handlers, into yet another subprocess.

Intermediate events on a subprocess border are another exception of an exception flow. Exception flow can be merged with the normal sequence flow after the subprocess. It is not always necessary, however, to merge exception flow with the normal flow. Figure 3–17 shows a Timer event with an exception flow that does not merge with the normal flow. The timer catches an event that may not have stopped the normal flow from executing. For instance, after two days we escalate the transaction to a manager.

In contrast, the intermediate error event in Figure 3–18 produces an exception flow that merges with normal flow. Here, the subprocess activities have stopped. To continue the process, the flows must merge. We recommend merging these flows with an exclusive data-based gateway. The implicit merge does not clearly identify the sole path taken.

Consider the flow when the exception flow implicitly merges from the Timer intermediate event. This could cause the "Pre-process" task to occur more than once because of the merging parallel condition.

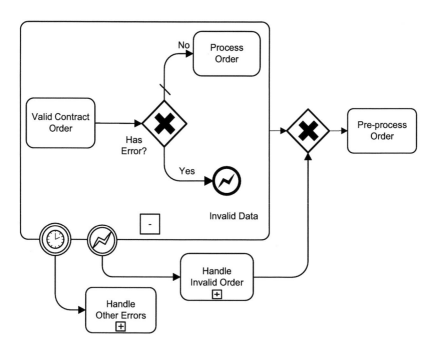

Figure 3–18   *If the process should continue after the exception, then merge the process.*

Compensation Events

There are four BPMN symbols for compensation events, as shown here.

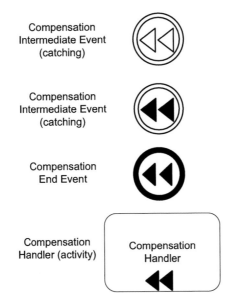

Compensation
Intermediate Event
(catching)

Compensation
Intermediate Event
(catching)

Compensation
End Event

Compensation
Handler (activity)

Compensation
Handler

Some activities create a specific output, or a committing of data that may need reversal if it is determined that a transaction should not proceed. The Compensation event and Compensation handling activities are used for this scenario. Compensation events are not used as part of process flow. Instead, Compensation shapes use the association line. A Compensation handler activity is an automatic activity that activates when a compensation event is thrown. A Compensation handler activity can be a single task, or it can be a subprocess when multiple rollback steps are required for a transaction.

Processes often create groups of transactions, in databases or application services, called nested transactions. A set or nesting of these transactions is called a savepoint. In rollbacks, transactions at a savepoint are removed. The Compensation event shapes include the intermediate Compensation event and the Compensation end event. You specify a Compensation condition with a pair: an end Compensation and an intermediate Compensation connected to a subprocess.

There is no Compensation start event. Like the Error event, you cannot start a process with a Compensation event. Optionally, the Compensation end event shape can signify a distributed transaction rollback. Use of the Compensation end event is an explicit way of causing compensation. Compensation events can also be implicit within the scope of a transaction. If a transaction were to fail, all Compensation handlers within a transaction subprocess should automatically start the rollback steps associated with each activity inside the transaction. Subprocesses

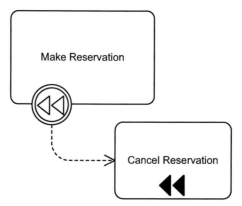

Figure 3–19   *Compensation intermediate event and an associated Compensation handler task.*

that illustrate a transaction should use a double line instead of the normal single line, rounded rectangle shape.

BPMN treats each subprocess as a separate, long-running transaction. The transaction records all sequences of activities. Because transactions in a business process approach might require long periods of time to complete, traditional mechanisms for saving database data are not always applicable. As the process executes, data might be saved to one or more (even many) databases. The idea of the long-running transaction relies on grouping these databases into smaller transaction sets. Therefore, your process will need the ability to undo the effects of a process that fails to complete.

Compensation handlers reverse the effect of a finished unit of work in a business process. However, because a process is not aware of the details of a database transaction, you will need to specify how the reversal happens. The process invokes the compensation when an error or unexpected condition arises during the normal work of the process. This cleans up the process for the Compensation handler to start its reversal activity.

As an example, suppose I want to have a peanut butter and jelly sandwich. I can't make this sandwich unless I have peanut butter, jelly, and bread. I won't know that I don't have the three items required until I go to retrieve the items. If I don't have all the required items, then I must return the other items. Errors might occur in this scenario, such as the bread being stale.

In Figure 3–20, you either associate each activity with an inverse action when the transaction fails, or you use a subprocess to handle all compensation in one handler activity. Either way, the association dotted line is used instead of the sequence flow solid line. Individual compensation handlers were used in this case because each activity required a specialized inverse activity to compensate for the transaction failure.

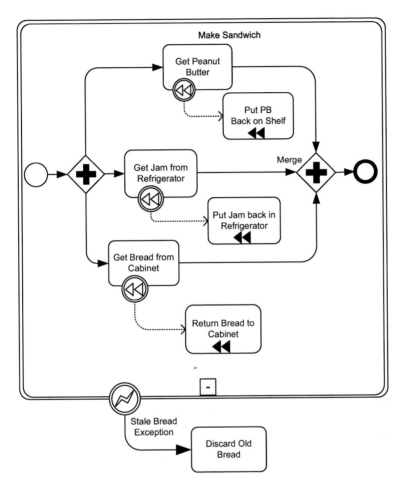

Figure 3–20 *Transaction subprocess containing Compensation events and associated Compensation handler activities.*

Cancel Events

The two Cancel events, the intermediate and end, are shown left to right.

The Cancel events are used with a subprocess that processes a transaction. There are only two types—the Cancel end event that throws the condition and the Cancel intermediate event that catches the condition. The Cancel intermediate event can only be placed on the border of a subprocess.

The Cancel end event is used when a condition is discovered that does not require compensation, but will cause the transaction to cancel. In Figure 3–21, we show the proper usage of the Cancel event shapes. When we try to update a database record that does not exist, we simply cancel the transaction.

Use the Cancel event properly and do not confuse it with Compensation events. Compensations back out transactions with reverse steps where data is partially written.

The Cancel end event is similar to the Terminate event. The cancel event, however, does not terminate the entire process—just the surrounding subprocess. If your intention is to stop all activities in the entire participant pool, use the Terminate event instead.

Figure 3–22 shows the combined use of Cancel and Compensation. An activity inside the transaction subprocess requires compensation when the transaction fails or cancels. The Cancel end event throws, and the Cancel intermediate event on the subprocess border catches.

The sequence flow from the Cancel intermediate event leads to an exception flow that notifies the customer, then cancels the entire process with the Terminate event. Because the compensation handler is inside a transaction subprocess, the Compensation should automatically take place if the transaction is rolled back. A Compensation end event could be used in place of the Cancel end event, but this only allows one activity to be associated with compensation. All other intermediate catching events allow for sequence flow.

Conditional Events

There are two Conditional events—the Conditional start event (*left*) and the Conditional intermediate event (*right*):

The Conditional event is equivalent to a message broadcast with a defined condition in the data. The condition evaluates message data and maps to a business concept. For instance, a process might start when payments are late on an invoice. Another process might await the completion of a user form. In either case, the participant monitoring a condition is decoupled from the other participants and is capable of acting on its own without being triggered.

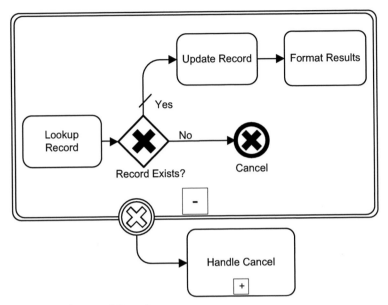

Figure 3–21   *The use of Cancel events.*

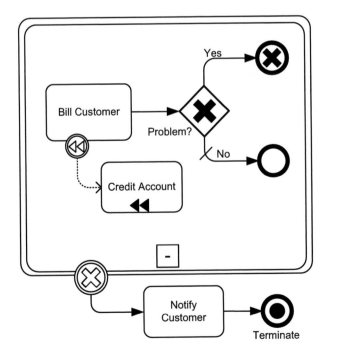

Figure 3–22   *Combined usage of Cancel, Compensation, and Terminate events.*

The Conditional event is used when a participant is actively monitoring data. For example, a participant monitors a file system for a specific file type to start the rest of the process (Figure 3–23). Another example is a security guard that stands watchfully doing nothing until trouble is spotted. Specify the represented condition with a descriptive label or a text annotation.

Link Event

The two types of Link events, intermediate catching (*left*) and throwing (*right*),[1] are shown here.

The Link event allows a diagram to continue onto another page. It is never a start event or an end event. If a diagram page is to start with a Link event, then use the catching (unfilled) intermediate Link event. If you want to continue the diagram on the next page, use the throwing intermediate Link event.

Processes cannot start with a link from another page because the process is already started. The Link shape marks a continuation point of an already running

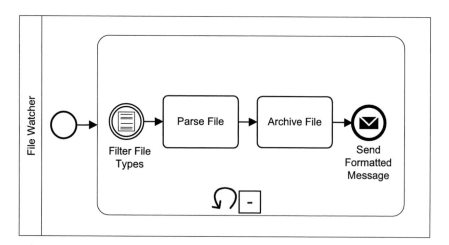

Figure 3–23   *Diagram of a file-system watcher that responds to a specific file type.*

---

1. In the BPMN 1.0 specification, there was also a Link start and Link end event. The BPMN 1.1 specification removed the Link start and Link end event.

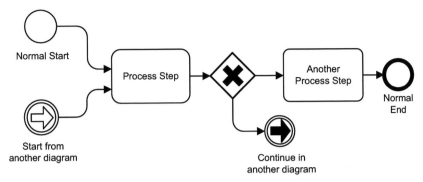

Figure 3–24 *Link event usage.*

process. You cannot end a process by linking to another point in the process. Once the process is done, it cannot resume. Therefore, only the intermediate Link shapes make sense.

Figure 3–24 shows the proper usage of the Link events. The process can be started by any start event. Alternately, the process can start with the intermediate Link event (catching). The gateway makes a decision to either continue in this diagram or continue on another diagram with the intermediate Link event (throwing).

Signal Event

Signal events are depicted by triangles inside circles. There are four types of signal events and corresponding symbols, as shown here.

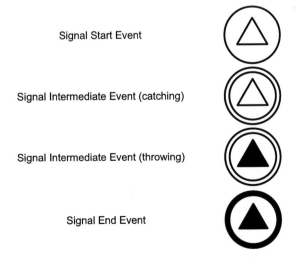

Signal shapes send a message from one participant to another. The process might send messages to a group of listening participants, or the group might even be indefinite. The signal pattern is like a radio broadcast. The message continuously broadcasts, and those who choose to listen to the broadcast tune in or subscribe.

The Signal event can broadcast to all processes simultaneously. The Signal intermediate (throwing) and Signal end shapes depict this broadcast. The Signal start and Signal intermediate (catching) events allow you to receive a broadcast.

The process in Figure 3–25 uses the Signal intermediate events as a stock symbol monitor. When the stock market opens, the process starts. The market opening bell signal is sent to all subscribing participants. After the stock market opens, the process watches for a price change greater than 10 percent. If a price change is detected, either a high or low stock alert will be broadcast to all other subscribing process participants.

Figure 3–26 shows a busy intersection from the perspective of three participants—a northbound driver, a westbound driver, and the traffic light that helps the two drivers avoid a collision. Drivers entering the intersection decide whether or not to proceed based on the color of the traffic light. The driver observes the traffic light and decides. Because the traffic light occurs during normal driving, the traffic signal light is a driver's Signal event. The stopped driver proceeds through the intersection if there is a green signal. From the perspective of the traffic light, a green signal is sent to traffic waiting at a red light.

The process in Figure 3–26 contrasts the Condition and Signal events. In the event gateway in the Condition event shape, participants actively monitor for a condition. With the Signal event shape, participants observe a broadcast message, while the Condition event is passively observed. The driver subscribes to the signal event and waits for it. The signal event is received by anyone within view of the traffic light (the subscribers). Without participants there is no explicit message interaction. Instead of using interaction lines, Figure 3–26 uses the group shape to illustrate the relationship between the signal throw and catch events. The usage of the Group shape is not mandatory—it just makes the diagram easier to read.

Figure 3–26 illustrates what happens after the signal change. The northbound driver is careless and hits the accelerator pedal. The westbound driver is more cautious and watches for crossing traffic even though the traffic light signals green. When a speeding driver crosses with disregard to the red signal, an error handling subprocess is managed with this exception condition.

This is an example of how easy it is to illustrate a complex interaction using just a few BPMN shapes. In fact, if we were to completely write out the entire scenario in text, there would likely be three or four pages. This small diagram shows the perspective of three participants, what they do, and how each action relates to the other participants.

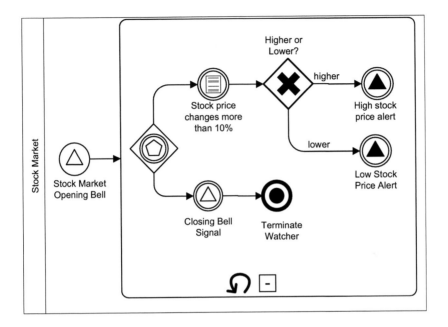

Figure 3–25 *Stock symbol monitor with signals.*

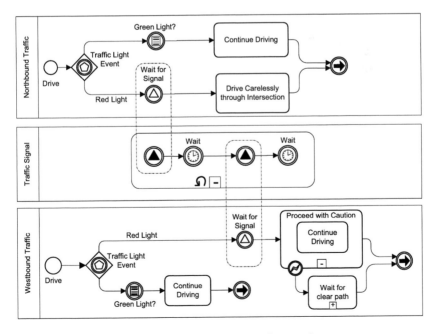

Figure 3–26 *Traffic light diagram using the Signal event shapes.*

SHAPES NOT COVERED (AND WHY)

Some BPMN shapes might not be very useful in a real-world scenario. For example, there is a multievent shape for an event triggered by any event type. Because it can be misinterpreted, we do not recommend that you use this type of notation. This is also true with the complex merge gateway. It allows any type of split to merge with one generic shape. If you remember the explanation of the gateway shapes, we suggested you should merge with the starting gateway shape. That said, Table 3–1 lists some of the shapes we do *not* recommend using.

SUMMARY

BPMN is simultaneously simple and complex as a diagramming language. The simplicity is that all shapes derive from the basic rectangle, circle, and diamond, yet there are enough shapes to describe very complex behavior while minimizing the descriptive text. This is the first diagramming language that we have found to be simple enough for the highest level diagrams, yet robust enough to describe very complex scenarios.

Previous attempts to create such a language have resulted in multiple flavors of the specification. For example, UML includes over a dozen diagram types. The creator of a BPMN diagram has the choice of illustrating the simple or the complex version of a process, but the notation set is the same for all diagrams. BPMN might illustrate someone's thought process as they walk down the street, or it might illustrate complex inner workings of software code. A BPMN diagram might illustrate one of the archetypes from the introduction, or you can use BPMN to illustrate flow in a data warehouse. In the next two chapters, we will explore more ways to model your business processes.

Table 3–1   Shapes We Do Not Recommend Using and Why

Shape Name	Shape	Purpose / Problem
Multiple Event		Indicates that multiple events trigger this shape. The implementation relies on a runtime engine to execute script or code, therefore the behavior is completely hidden from the diagram. This is useful if you like to write code, but not as useful if you want to effectively communicate with a diagram. Try using the exclusive event-driven gateway with specific event shapes instead.
Complex Merge		Indicates that there are multiple ways to merge flow paths on this shape. While this may seem like a nice shortcut to solve your merge problems, it may introduce interpretation errors and unpredictable merge behavior. Instead, stick to the rule "if you split with it, merge with it." You can also try using a subprocess shape to merge paths that don't seem to match up.
Empty Gateway		According to the BPMN specification, this shape is identical to the exclusive gateway. We don't recommend using it because you are inviting interpretation error. Being more explicit is always better for accurate communication.
Event Driven Gateway (BPMN 1.0)		This is an older version of the event-driven gateway. There are rules restricting this shape so that all attached intermediate events must be identical. The newer 1.1 version (pentagon instead of six-sided star) allows for any intermediate event combination to be attached.
Link Start Event		Signals that the process starts from another page. This does not make sense because if it's already started it cannot start here. Use the Link intermediate (catching) event instead.
Link End Event		Signals that the process ends here but can continue on another page. This doesn't make sense because if the process ends, it cannot continue. Use the Link intermediate (throwing) event instead .

CHAPTER 4

GATHERING REQUIREMENTS
WITH BPMN

INTRODUCTION

When you model your processes in BPMN, your firm will move from the loosely defined use case to a hierarchy of process models such as described in the Process Modeling Framework (PMF). Most use cases mix the PMF steps of process phase modeling and scenario modeling. In this chapter, we present a means for improving this.

MODELING MATURITY

In process modeling, your organization likely seeks improved performance and alignment or re-engineered processes. More often, it is the decisions that need improvement. In the introduction, we described the five layers of a BPMN process modeling framework (PMF). In the first layer, core process activities and flows are modeled. In the next, critical decisions are identified. Through increased and detailed process modeling, increased understanding arises. We suggest you start process modeling by defining core business processes.

In your Joint Application Design (JAD) sessions, firms often make "happy days"[1] use case scenarios, business modeling, or creating workflow diagrams in Visio, or combinations of these. These use cases (and business cases) haphazardly gather more (or less) information than defined in the PMF. A use case approach often models too many details of the process—from the core level through workflow scenario. The implication, and our experience, is that this approach is too ambitious and leads to uneven and unpredictable results. Process steps are con-

---

1. The term "happy days" refers to an analysis that only considers the process when all conditions are favorable.

fused with business rules. There is a tendency to cling to old, batch-oriented patterns. JAD participants become bored and frustrated.

A "happy day" path only considers flows that occur when the process manages no exceptions. You can take this approach by focusing on activities, gateways, and flows. Therefore, someday your team should visit "unhappy" branches. Converting the use case or work flow into the formal needs of a business process model in BPMN can be challenging.

As your organization becomes more mature in the use of BPM, you will create process models directly in business process modeling notation (BPMN). Beyond the core business process, these JAD sessions are primarily working on process and scenario modeling in the PMF. As your experience grows, your firm will probably separate the use case scenarios into these levels.

Business analysts should become process analysts who build executable processes with BPMN in the PMF. Until then, you need an approach to translate the use case or Visio diagrams into an accurate BPMN model of these workflows. You might convert existing use cases into BPMN, or you might transition the organization to a BPMN. This chapter offers simple guidelines for both.

If your goal is to digitize a process, then moving a use case into a BPM prepares the way for model execution, i.e., moving a use case through the layers of the PMF. The activities described in this chapter help this transition.

From Use Case to BPMN

To envisage a practical approach to designing processes from a use case document, we should review the main terms. These definitions guide a translation from a use case to a process design. We already defined a business process as an event-activated flow of decision-coordinated activities, conducted by participants and acting on data, information, and knowledge that achieves a goal. We covered these important terms in the two chapters on BPMN. Consider the features of a use case:

- An event, a circle-enclosed shape—timing words (when, until, while) describing or marking an event.
- A flow, a line, and an arrow shape—the use case should suggest motions of data from activity to activity or participant to participant.
- Data owned by a business process might not be extensively described in the use case. However, a competent process analyst can intuit many attributes from the description.
- A business decision is the outcome of business rules applied to process information. Use cases do not clearly define the decision, and business rules point to decisions.

- An activity, a rounded rectangle shape—the use case will describe the tasks performed. Often a single sentence describes several messages, activities and participants.

- A participant is the lane shape within a pool. The use case is written from an actor's perspective.

- The goal is the final state or aim of the process. A thorough use case should explain what the interaction hopes to achieve.

The task is to parse the semantics of the use case into core design components (BPMN) of the business process. The challenge of the "happy days" use case is that it is not always obvious what should be an activity, event, participant, flow, or decision. Furthermore, as suggested in the BPMN basics, design decisions arise from the use case: What type of gateway? Should it be parallel or sequential?

To parse our use case semantics, we form a map from the use case sentence into one or more of the process components defined earlier. We also simplify the diagram by setting business rules apart from process activities. A logic tree expresses the details of elements of the decision that may be hidden in BPMN.

Use cases that expound on business rules are often set up in computer code in the Software Development Life Cycle (SDLC). Business rules management systems automate changes in the details of the logic tree. For instance, business rules might apply to a new customer segment. Most BPMN tools cannot add or drop process activities and gateways in response to a controlling event—you must manually redeploy the process diagram's logic. Avoid encoding business rules in the process or computer code so that the decision is understandable and flexible.

Deciding Business Rules and Process Requirements

You can develop any complex business rule in BPMN. It is unnecessary, however, to convert every use case sentence into a BPMN. Business rules should be visually expressed as truth tables or logic trees. The truth table is a two-dimensional expression of conditions and conclusions. An entire truth table or logic tree can be expressed in BPMN, but this would be a poor use of that tool. Business rules should be a service for decisions within the process. This is an industry best practice. If your BPMN diagrams reflect too many business rules, then they will become unnecessarily complicated.

Positioning the business rule for change is a key benefit of using business rules. Rules can affect multiple decisions, so your process modeling activity should include a rules approach. This is another industry best practice. Rules must be properly designed to avoid unintended side affects. That is, changing a rule in your Business Rules Management System (BRMS) should predictably affect process outcome.

The choice of what should become a business rule and what becomes a part of the process is not difficult. The business rule should support a decision and the process should direct the data to the services that consume or provide data. Consider the following design items and guidelines in Table 4–1 for what to carry out as business rules and what BPMN to include on the process diagram.

The business rule should evaluate the data the process provides. A business rule can set one or more process parameters or attributes, and then the process should apply the parameter to a BPM decision. The BPMN diagram is often a complex map of flow control. It will have many subprocesses, decisions and "while loops." Wherever a decision or while loop appears, you should consider it the basis for the change in flow. This is the best use of business rules in the business process.

The last three examples are "gray areas." If you are gaining reference data changes for a process and this reference data provides important process parameters for decisions, then you should consider this a business rule. If the reference data are process data for gateways, sequencing, or timing events, then you might not need the business rules approach. A business rule can map process data for interfaces. If the systems support group must update many contortions of the interface's data, then a business rule might be an effective way of managing this.

Finally, if systems outside the business process environment need data, then either business rules engines or business process engines can store operational data. Your process analysts decide this in the latter phases of the PMF.

Process Decisions

As implied above, most business processes contain multiple decision points. Processes decide what discounts to offer customers, what benefits apply to an insurance customer, or which mode of transportation to use to ship a product. At these decision points, logic evaluates the data in the process. These are the business rules that support the decision. If you change the business rule, you will change the process's behavior.

Decisions drive the process, but the decision may be comprised of many business rules. For instance, there are many computations and queries needed to decide what is covered by drug therapy in a health insurance policy. Drug therapies are decided by the customer policy type, state regulations, and available, efficient alternatives. In simple terms, the decision encapsulates the business process's intellectual logic.

The decision is an expression of business policy. It must be easily understood by the business. Business rules are how business policy is enforced by the process. As the business policy changes, the business rules underlying the decisions also change. The decision process remains the same. The process uses a sequence of activities (the process requests several decisions) and gateways that direct the decision.

We have some simple guidelines for those activities or flow control branches that should be in the BRMS. Consider the process fragment shown in Figure 4–1.

Table 4–1   Guidelines for Rules and BPMN

Design Item	Example	BPMN or Rule
Logic statement	If Customer is preferred, then develop greatest discount	Rules engine, business rule, truth tables
Policy	When Customers are denied coverage in the state of California…	Business rule, truth tables, and logic trees
Post to application service	SAP PM®	Business process participant, pool shape
State, duration, or location of entity	Car assigned to Customer, payment is late	Business process event shape
Direct data to branch of process	Process decision, while loop, subprocess	Business process gateway
Read external transaction	Customer requisition on product delivery contract	Business process participant
Certify external transaction	Confirm attributes of a transaction	Business rule, logic tree
Report data errors to external system	Errors in business rule approval	Business process activity
Reference data	Customer's credit limit	Business rule logic tree or business process
Convert process data to interface	Mapping accounting transactions for ERP	Business rule or business process participant, activity
Store data in operational data store	Record the clerical details of an order	Business rule logic tree or business process activity

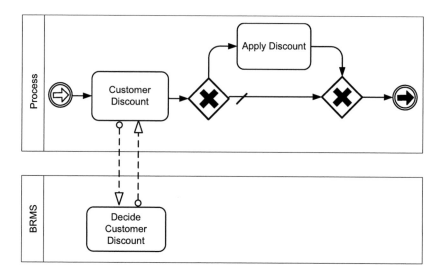

Figure 4–1   *Decision gateway for applying customer discount. The business rules that decide the customer discount should not be included in the BPMN.*

Figure 4–1 shows a decision for a discount as applied to a customer order when one exists. The decision in the process is the selected discount. Discounts and incentives on purchases is a widespread practice designed to motivate customer behavior. A company might manage many business rules about customer discounts. For example,

- Customers with more than $10,000 in orders shall receive a 5% discount on purchases.
- Customers with between $5,000 and $10,000 in orders shall receive a 3% discount.
- Customers with a negotiated discount shall receive the discount.
- Customers who live in a particular zip code shall receive a local discount.

The list could go on and on. A BPMN setting up these rules might appear as shown in Figure 4–2.

Businesses often rapidly change the business rules associated with decisions like a customer discount. The changes might be mandated by a review or "governance" process, or they might be the outcome of decision analytics. Decision analytics tools can add and delete branches in the computations shown in Figure 4–2. Also, the BPM industry has shown improved productivities using business rules approaches. Business rules are a clear expression of the steps that support a decision process. Our customer discount example from Figure 4–2 is best expressed in the decision table shown in Table 4–2.

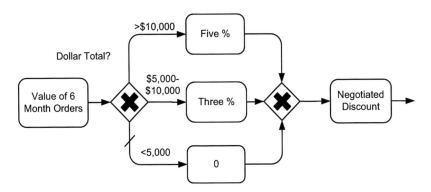

Figure 4–2 *Some business rules in BPMN, governing a discount decision. This is an example of the wrong approach: the business rules are mixed up with the process.*

Table 4–2 Business Rules from Figure 4–2 in Truth-Table Format

Recent Purchases	Negotiated Discount	BPMN or Rule
>$10,000	N/A	5%
>$5,000 - <= $10,000	N/A	3.5%
a	YES	%Value
Etc...	...	...

a   is a wildcard character.

Decision analytics is a statistical analysis of the policies expressed in the business rules of the truth table. An outcome might suggest adding a small discount for customers whose purchases are between $3,000 and $5,000. With a business rules approach, this is a simple matter.

The *requirements* of the customer order process are the proper discounts applied according to company policies. The truth table row with 5% discounts for customers buying more than $10,000 is not a requirement of the use case. The 5% discount is data just as the customer's address is data.

Before gathering process requirements, we suggest you decide how business rules will be designed. Because the rules that support the decision in Figure 4–2 and Table 4–2 often change, using a business rules approach will simplify the harvesting of business rules and offers more execution agility. It is poor practice to model business rules in BPMN as shown in Figure 4–2. There are many IT industry studies that support this position.

The decision is the best point for evaluation of performance by collecting and assessing business performance metrics. It is also a good point for limiting the extent of use case steps that become a part of the business process.

Defining Participant, Activity, and Flow

A use case is an ordered sequence of action descriptions. Action descriptions are complete sentences and should be in the following form:

Subject … Verb… Direct object … Prepositional phrase

Parsing the sentence for the participant should be simple—the participant is the subject and the activity becomes the verb and perhaps part of the remaining phrase. In BPMN, the participant defines a swim lane and activity rectangles. This is not always obvious from every action description, however, especially from business rules or decisions.

As covered in the Chapter 2, "BPMN: Basics and Gateways," a flow (a solid arrow in BPMN) is a sequence from one activity to the next in the same swim lane. A message is a flow of data from one participant's activity to another participant's activity (from one swim lane to another). BPMN shows that message as a dotted arrow. Be aware that flows or messages can be presented as all or a portion of the activity in the use case sentence. For instance, consider these use case action description sentences:

1. Requisition Officer selects the Order Type.
2. Requisition Officer requests a Quotation for Transport from Vendor.
3. The Transport vendor reviews…
4. The Requisition Officer approves the Transport when the Quote is less than 10% greater than the acceptable price.

With the reasoning above, the second sentence of the use case becomes
- Participant: Requisition Officer
- Activity: Request a Quotation
- A message to the Vendor
- Participant: Vendor
- Event Receive Request

The BPM notation shows something similar to that of Figure 4–3. For each sentence, consider the participant. Is the first event (thin circle) the start of the participant's process? Is it the last event (thick circle)? Consider the activity and event. Is your participant actively preparing data, inspecting information, and deciding among choices (gateway) in the use case? Again consider the second sentence of the use case. Since we need a transportation quotation, we need a transportation vendor process and a message to that process.

Figure 4–3 shows the BPMN fragments for the use case fragment. Obviously, use case sentences and BPMN symbols do not agree one-to-one. Consider the fourth sentence in our use case fragment: "The Requisition Officer approves the Transport when ..." It has at least one activity, three transitions, and two gateways. Besides, the use case seems incomplete. What would happen when the transportation quote is inadequate? Figure 4–4 shows the BPMN fragment for the fourth sentence.

Two Important BPMN Patterns for Use Cases

Use case sentences often fall into a common pattern: activity, message, gateway, (to completion). A frequent use of the pattern is to gather information from another participant, then decide how to proceed.

The sentences are

- The actor action verb message from the system.
- If (when) condition one, then option one ...
- If (when) condition two, then option two ...

Business case examples are

- The grant applicant requests funding approval from the research division.
- If the request is approved, the grant applicant creates a project folder.
- If the research division request more information, then ...

Another one is

- The requisition officer requests a special delivery of fuel to the airport.
- If the due date of the requisition's delivery is more than the latest acceptable date then the requisition officer reports to the flight commander.
- The requisition clerk approves the special delivery.

The BPMN for this pattern is shown in Figure 4–6.

Looping in a Condition

In this pattern, the actor performs activities during a condition. It can also be used to suspend activities until another activity occurs or there are three types of loops (while, for each, and until).

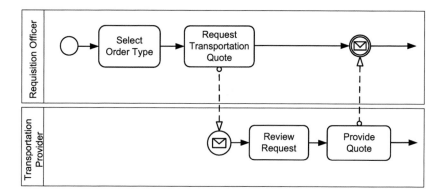

Figure 4–3   *Steps 1 through 4 of the use case fragment.*

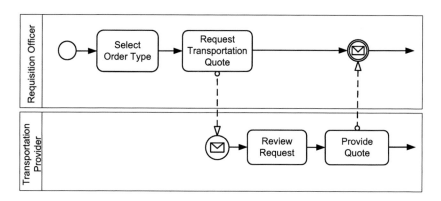

Figure 4–4   *Steps 1 through 4 of the use case fragment.*

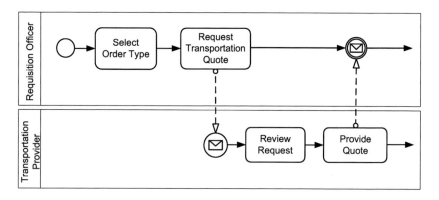

Figure 4–5   *Steps 1 through 4 of the use case fragment.*

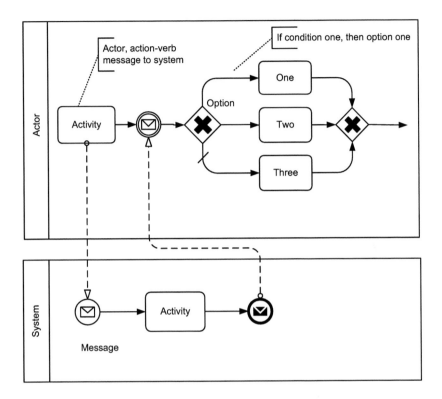

Figure 4–6   *Simple pattern: one activity-message-activity.*

The sentence is

Looping preposition, condition description, actor action verb.

Business case examples are

- While the construction activity occurs, the inspector monitors material and activities' compliance with specifications.
- For each email application received, a sales representative reviews customer details and creates a project folder.

The BPMN for this pattern is shown in Figure 4–7.

Note: The BPMN of the condition for this pattern need not be mentioned as shown in the "direct check." Standard attributes in the BPMN specification define the condition and a process instance automatically monitors. A direct check is sometimes expedient for clarity.

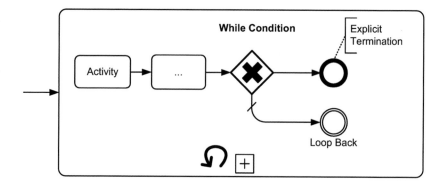

Figure 4–7 *Simple pattern: a while check with a direct check for the condition.*

For the first two levels in the BPMN framework, these two patterns will suit most circumstances found in use cases. Beware of looping prepositions such as *while, when,* and *at the same time*. They may point out parallel activities, not looping.

Deciding Sequential, Parallel, and Looping Activities

Timing sentences can suggest activities that occur in parallel in the same participant or another participant. Timing words such as "while," "during," and "until" imply either parallel or looping activities. Use case designers should consider what should be parallel and what should be sequential. Parallel activities are activities that take place at the same time. Parallel activities in multiple participants are coordinated by completion messages or event gateways.

A use case can call out parallel activities plainly or implicitly. Use case sentences might refer to a subprocess by a term or set of related terms. Alternatively, a parallel activity might be designed for efficiency.

Consider the following sentences:

- While **subprocess A and subprocess B** occur, **actor** X activity, another activity.
- When **subprocess A and subprocess B** are complete, then actor X activity.

You might imagine subprocess A and subprocess B are services that the central process need. For instance, one could provide a transportation quotation and another could provide a manufacturing date. The "and" proscribes actor X's process awaiting both subprocesses to complete. Often these two subprocesses are providing data the process needs. This is another circumstance where you should exercise care in translating the use case into an explicit merge. The solution for the "and" circumstance is shown in Figure 4–8.

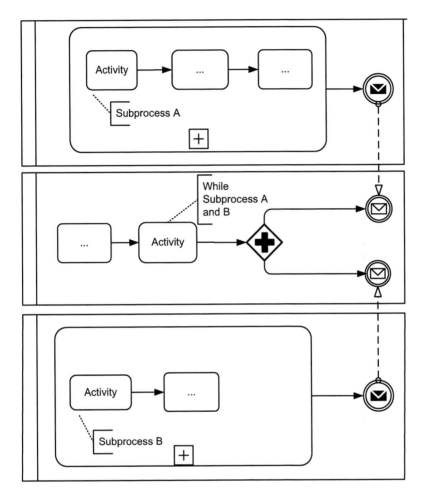

Figure 4–8 *This is a diagram fragment. The activity in the center awaits the two subprocesses. The need for both subprocesses infers an explicit parallel merge.*

Figure 4–8 displays the proper use of the intermediate messages and parallel gateways. There are more notations: an "or" in the sentence would proscribe an actor's process waiting for one of the subprocesses to complete. This would not be the usual.

The outcome of this modeling would be a rigorous definition of the core business processes, plus the "core process" phase as suggested by the process modeling framework.

Finding the Decision and Separating the Decision from the Rule

Business rules should identify decisions in the use case. Business rules can be categorizations, computations, comparisons, and controls (called C^4) that branch activities or make a determination about a fact within the process. The question to ask is, "Is this use case 'requirement' creating or computing data for latter use in a process gateway?" If you have already modeled the process, are many gateways grouped and closely connected? Rules discovered in use cases should be relegated to the business rules approach. Workflow diagrams that include business rules might display a sequence of data-exclusive diamonds converging on the decision. In use case action statements, we detect decisions or business rule activities by asking the following:

- Does the action validate, verify or confirm information in the process?
- Does the verb decide, direct or control the flow?
- Does the action compute values for use in a latter comparison? For instance, does the action compute a value that defines a change in direction later in the use case?
- Does the action divert the flow of the use case based on a previously decided proposition?

These questions suggest sentences in the use case that might be business rules. As we have suggested, the business rule should not be a part of the process model, only the decision.

More Tests for Business Rules

Arguably, every business rule can be expressed in formal logic: "If *condition, condition,* ... then *conclusion.*" In the condition part of the business logic, business rules classify, calculate, and compare. The decision part is the control.

Business rules do the following:

> **Classify** the type, the division, and the sort. Firms classify multiple types of customers: eligible, ineligible, delinquent, preferred, and others. A business rule often starts by filtering exactly what it is deciding.
>
> **Calculate** and compute formulas, look up data and statistics, and transform and assign values. Constraints are often numerical. How long has the customer been covered? How much of the deductible amount do we extend to the customer? This classification includes queries in the computation.

Compare the calculation to the redline. The redline is a key value that must be reached, or not exceeded, or within a specified range.

Control what is true, valid, correct, or mistaken, and the messages that go with them. This is what the process does as shown in Figure 4–6. Policies are often qualitative: insurance companies need many controls on the benefits extended to customers.

With all these parts, a business rules method develops process decisions. Of all the C's, the most critical part of a business rule is the red lines and thresholds of Compare. These are the turning points of the decision and trigger process control. If the value of a calculation is above, below, or within a threshold, then the rule accepts or rejects. Sometimes the threshold is a list. Imagine a status flag that stands for a failed or broken item. There might be several of these that managers can change when there is a change in policies.

In your business case, or use case, business rules might sequentially validate information. A validation is a sequence of logic that evaluates to true or false. You use validations to decide if a condition—such as the completeness and relevance of information in a customer claim—has been met. Rules might also look up data as in a transformation. A transformation computes and assigns values to data in your use case. For instance, you might use a transformation to look up a benefit for a customer, control a customer discount, or look up a status. Processes enforce corporate policies and governance with decisions supported by validation and transformation business rules.

Business Rules Examples

We suggest you examine your use case and parse the statement for participants, activities, flows, and events that become part of a process model. Business rules should be managed separately. If you carefully read (or listen to) your use case, you should be able to identify business rules and the decisions they support. The forth C in C^4 is control. Control can be a process decision or a part of a process decision.

For example, the statement "The contract system should deny a requisition for a direct delivery contract whose period of performance ends within 15 days"

- Classifies the contract, or qualifies the statement, as a direct delivery contract.
- Computes (or needs the computation of) the period of performance.
- Compares the period of performance and a 15-day period.
- Controls or decides when to deny the requisition.

The statement "Customers with more than three accidents in the past three years are ineligible for coverage"

- Classifies the entity as a customer.
- Computes the number of accidents in the past three years.
- Compares that number with the scalar number 3.
- Controls or decides the eligibility for coverage.

Use cases will often describe many rules that approve or deny a requisition or control the eligibility for coverage. These statements can be gathered into a "fact table." In modeling processes, however, it is efficient to use them to identify the decision point.

Steps to Execution

In this short book, we have covered some of the steps that move a use case or business conversation closer to a form that can be executed. We have not covered the critical steps of process engineering and data modeling. Data is critical to developing a process prototype. This is an activity that can be done in parallel with use case development and conversion to the data model. Complete process models need orchestration and choreography. Engineering the solution requires an understanding of the types of choreography and orchestration for the considered problem domain.

SUMMARY

If your organization is working with a portfolio of process projects, you should decide your approach to business rules. With a nondiagrammatic approach to business rules, and a meeting of executives and directors, your process projects should not get deeper than the "Phases of the Process" detail. This is described in the process modeling foundation in this book's introduction, where major activities and decisions are described.

Process models produced by this technique are acceptable for communicating an understanding of a process. You might consider process improvements at this point.

We identified some simple BPMN patterns that you can use to parse most use case (and business case) sentences. These include the following:

> **Activity, message, gateway (to completion):** The most frequent use of the pattern is to gather information from another participant and then decide what to do with the information.

Looping in a condition: In this pattern, the actor performs activities during a condition. It can also be used to perform activities until completion or until another participant has completed.

For the first two levels in the BPMN framework, these two patterns will suit most circumstances faced in use cases.

As your project becomes more detailed, meetings can focus on business analysts and subject matter experts. The PMF suggest separate methods for gathering workflow scenarios and business rules. Your team can separate workflow requirements from the business rules requirements with a combination of the suggestions in Table 4–1.

CHAPTER 5

PATTERNS: BPMN FOR
COMBINING WORKFLOWS

PROCESS AND EXECUTION

In the requirements chapter, we described how your process team can parse the sentences of business conversation into a set of activities, events, and flows in BPMN. Generally, the business conversations among managers and SMEs describe workflows over short time frames. For instance, you might model the customer approval portion of an order-to-cash process. As Figure 5–1 suggests, coordinating the output of three or more of these efforts requires effort. This chapter describes patterns of BPMN modeling solutions that solve these process requirements over longer time frames.

In the early phases of the PMF project, teams create core business processes and the phases of these processes with their core decisions. Later on, your team will discover coordination needs among groups of workflows over longer time periods. For example, your process might assign work to alternate offices. Sometimes, the process must choose among different categories, as in truck, airfreight, or rail for a transportation mode. The outcome of other processes drives these choices. Something has to schedule, run, and monitor these processes. This is an example of *process choreography*.

When many workflows and subprocesses converge or diverge, you need different tools and approaches for a technically accurate solution. You will need broader, more cross-process solutions. Process-oriented firms use common patterns to coordinate the outcome of different process modeling phases.

Process solutions break when there is a weak implementation of requirements. If you match the needs of coordinating many processes with the correct workflow solution, you can avoid painful reconstruction of processes. Workflow patterns are part of a technically sound business process design approach. We will discuss some patterns of solutions for coordinating workflow scenarios.

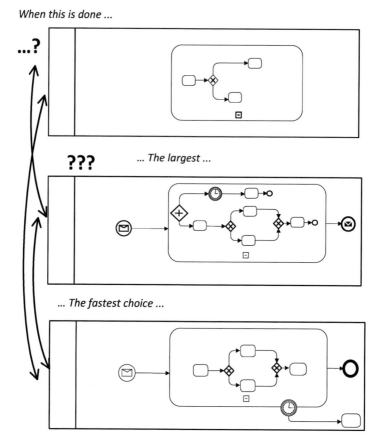

Figure 5–1   *Workflow patterns coordinate many workflows, and the dialogs of business conversations in JAD sessions decide the pattern.*

Patterns That Solve Real World Problems

When you study problem solving with an experienced practitioner, you learn an internal dialog for visualizing a problem. For instance, if you study data modeling, you learn an internal dialog for translating requirements into a picture of the data (entity relationship diagrams). Also, you might identify an intersection entity ("table between tables") as the result of shared, multiple relations between two entities. Other relations unfold as the modeling team "unpacks" and explores definitions. Simply put, the shape of the picture of the data flows from the dialog. Similarly, you select the correct workflow patterns from the dialog surrounding the choreography of workflows. Just as in data modeling, the patterns lay within the wording of the process requirement.

The benefit of applying patterns to your process problem is the assurance that your solution should be complete and run properly in the process engine.

Many patterns, especially the complex ones, are difficult to write with traditional programming techniques. By specifying your problem in process diagrams, the solution is left to the BPM engine and its evaluation of the BPMN, not the skill of the individual programmer.

Looping Approval Pattern

A frequently met workflow pattern is the approval of an employee's, customer's, or supplier's extraordinary request. The pattern's wording might be

> *The late, outstanding, overdue, or special request is approved by the manager. If more information is required, then the request is returned to the* employee, customer, *or* client.

Those requests might include "extraordinary" ERP business transactions from suppliers and trading partners. Defining a request as late, outstanding, overdue, or special is a decision that requires business rules. Assume the process has decided that a request (or a process) needs review or intervention. Next, a process participant (manager) evaluates the request and either approves or returns the request to the originating participant. We call this the *looping approval* pattern.

Examples of this pattern include

- Insurance claim verification.
- Employee absences of more than 12 days must be approved by their supervisor.
- Budget variance requests.
- Contract change orders exceed the contracting officers purchasing authority.

Sometimes a reviewer must approve all requests. The reviewer might also provide important data values to the attributes of a business object.

Another important decision assigns a reviewer to the request. If the request is complex, such as an insurance claim, then this pattern needs a work assignment or queuing process. We cover this pattern in the "Coordinating Many Choices" section in this chapter.

An Approval Process for the Workflow Scenario Phase

Figure 5–2 presents a model of the looping approval scenario, developed during the workflow scenario phase of your PMF. Here is a short description of the process:

1. In a subprocess, the submitter creates a request. If approval is needed, the request is sent to the Request System process. Next, the submitter

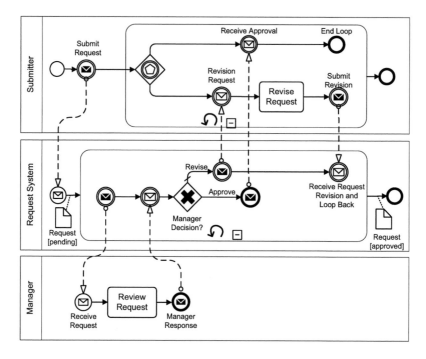

Figure 5–2 *BPMN for the looping approval pattern.*

instance will wait until the review is complete or not—thus, the event gateway.

2.   The approval process forwards the request to the approver or manager. The manager completes his/her review of the process.

3.   If the manager approves the request, the process tells the submitter. Otherwise, the submitter must revise the request. Since Steps 1 through 3 are repeated until the request is approved, a loop is explicit.

Not shown is a decision for deciding when the request needs approval. This is another opportunity for business rules to improve process productivity. If no approval is needed, then the scenario is complete.

The looping approval process displays the power of the workflow engine. An instance (or copy) of the submitted process is preserved until the approval loop is complete.

The elements of the pattern are

•   A request, transaction, or other data that might be approved. The submitter pool has elements of a workflow form or xml transaction.

- A decision to approve the request and business rules for this decision. A call to the rules engine decides when transactions are approved. This is not shown.
- A process that receives the request and loops between the approver and requestor until the approver is happy with the request.

Figure 5–2 presents an excellent example of the use of the event gateway in the submitter pool. The event gateway arises from parsing our problem semantics. From the submitter's view, there are two event possibilities—either the form is approved or more information is needed. A more complete design would include a timer on the loop.

Surveys, Marketing, and Feedback

Sometimes a process gathers data from an unknown number of participants. The pattern's wording might be "Request feedback from at least 20% of the customers" or "A minimum of 20 participants are required for the class to be scheduled."

The process does not know the number of instances of an activity at run time. We use this pattern when we don't know how many responses or instances of an activity will happen. Here, the process must wait until all instances are completed, then other activities will start. While some activities execute or are completed, new ones might often be created—your process might ask for more responses.

A Survey Process for the Workflow Scenario Phase

Figure 5–3 presents a model of the survey, marketing, or feedback scenario. In the example in Figure 5–3, an email invites a response from customers or actors in the process. The loop awaits a satisfactory response, as determined by a decision. This might be developed in the workflow scenario phase of the PMF. Here is a short description of the process:

1. An incoming message starts a survey. The "Email Recipients" task sends email to a mailing list.
2. The survey process loops for incoming email. The results of the survey are tallied by the "Survey Decision" activity, which calls business rules that decide the adequacy of the survey.
3. A gateway decides if the survey results are satisfactory. Usually, the gateway is optional. BPM tools specify the looping conditions.

Other examples of this pattern include

- Getting bids for work from multiple trading partners.
- Awaiting the delivery of multiple shipments from vendors to a facility before completing a process.

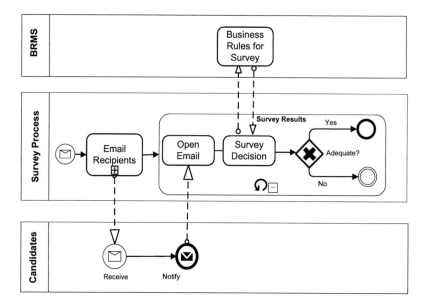

Figure 5–3   *BPMN for the survey, marketing or feedback pattern.*

You assign this pattern when the process must respond to multiple unknown quantities of events.

The elements of the pattern are

- A request from multiple sources by email, messaging, html, or other sources.
- A loop that awaits the arrival of information from these sources.
- A decision to approve the survey and business rules for this decision— a call to the rules engine to decide when the survey response is satisfactory.
- A process that receives the request and loops between the approver and requestor until the approver is happy with the request.

Coordinating Many Choices

Another common, advanced pattern occurs when the process chooses a path. The pattern's wording might be "Assign the insurance claim investigation to the nearest claims adjustor" or "Assign the design change request to next available, capable engineering team."

The technical name for this is *deferred choice*. This is a point in the business process where one of several branches is chosen. The choice is not made based on a business rule but from several offered alternatives. A decision classifies the alternate as acceptable. Business rules characterize the resources as "nearest available" or "next available." Only one of the decided alternatives is carried out. Once the process starts down the chosen branch, the other alternative branches are automatically withdrawn. The choice is called *deferred* because it is suspended until the processing in one of the alternative starts—that is, the choice is made as late as possible.

As with all patterns, there is a decision. Is the requested resource available? Business rules will decide if the customer's insurance adjustor is the nearest, or if the design team is capable.

A Survey Process for the Workflow Scenario Phase

In Figure 5–4, three routing switches are available to handle incoming message traffic. The top pool simultaneously requests the resources of one of the switches. As soon as one of the switches responds, the calling process assigns the workload to the switch and requests to the others are withdrawn. A more general solution would loop among a number of switches.

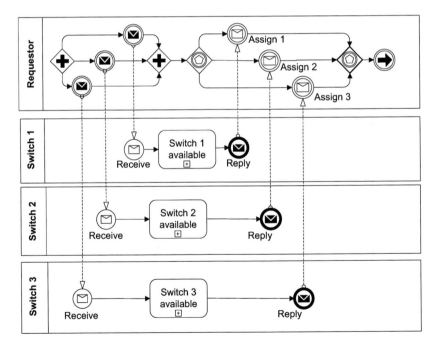

Figure 5–4 *The deferred choice pattern.*

Figure 5–4 uses several important BPMN features that reduce the amount of complicated computer programming. First, the requestor's message is automatically broadcast to the three switches. Once a resource responds, the other requests are automatically withdrawn. This is a feature of the event gateway; computer programs need not be written for this.

The elements of the pattern are

- An assignment of some work to a choice of resources. They might be labor pools, equipment queues, factories, or service representatives.
- A decision about resource availability.
- An event gateway in the original request that awaits the resource.

van der Aalst Patterns: Not a Business Tool

Oft-mentioned patterns are within the work of the Netherlands researcher Wil van der Aalst. Dr. van der Aalst and other researchers identified twenty-one workflow patterns that define the universe of possibilities that a "complete" workflow engine must address. The seminal paper, entitled *Workflow Patterns*, published in 2003, is readily available on the Internet. These patterns were not designed to solve business problems. They were designed to be complete in a theoretical sense. If a software workflow engine can run all the patterns, then the engine is certifiably complete.

Some of the patterns offer compact solutions to workflow patterns. We have used two of them in these patterns—deferred choice and "multiple instances without a prior run-time knowledge." Their descriptions, however, are technical and not focused on business problems. There are some complete BPMN solutions to the patterns on the Internet. One of the best is Steven White's *Process Modeling Notations and Workflow Patterns* (2004).

Some of the important van der Aalst workflow patterns that we have already discussed, with simple BPMN, include the following:

> **Synchronizing merge** is a pattern at a point where many subprocesses merge. As shown in Figure 5–5, the workflow *synchronizes* the output from all the incoming parallel paths. Therefore, the synchronizing merge pattern adds the inclusive parallel path shape to the BPMN specification.
>
> **Deferred choice** is the point where the process makes one of several choices from several alternates. In the process, it represents a point, as shown in Figure 5–6, where alternatives are based on an event that occurs at that point in the process. The deferred choice pattern also calls out the event gateway in the BPMN specification.

There are 19 more patterns that have technical names and different solutions in BPMN. Some match single BPMN shapes, others match configurations of sev-

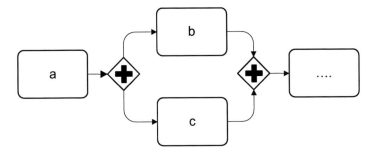

Figure 5–5   *BPMN for the synchronizing merge patterns.*

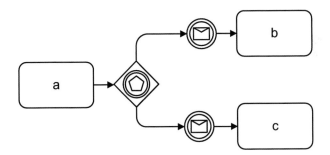

Figure 5–6   *BPMN for the deferred choice pattern.*

eral shapes. Understanding and knowing all of these is not compulsory for successful process modeling. What you should understand is that the workflow patterns created many of the BPMN shapes. The combinations of shapes create a powerful approach to workflow modeling.

Process Patterns Summary

As the BPM industry matures, and practitioners repeatedly create the same workflow patterns, more patterns and practices will emerge. All these patterns share two traits:

- A pivotal event—the merging of a known or unknown number of choices or the diverging of a known or unknown number of flows.
- A decision that defines a condition for the event and the choices.

Tools will become more powerful and process teams will become more adept. More abstract services will become available and process diagrams will become more expressive. Indeed, as we noted in Chapter 2, "BPMN: Basics and Gateways," even BPMN shapes have improved.

Developing processes with patterns improves the deep understanding of the final version, yet much of the important work remains. In a project modeling framework, you should consider simulating this development artifact in a test bed. Finally, the technical team should detail the process diagram with the necessary scheduling, exceptions, and compensations. The purpose of the details is to erect a more complete process model. The business processes should act on all the messages, including the system failures. The process should handle every expected exception.

THE MANAGING EXCEPTIONS SERVICE PHASE

In the last phases of a PMF, process engineers and technologists add more technical details to the process models. Many of these late details are process exceptions. As ensconced in ITIL or COBIT, standards proactively proscribe that failure for all processes should be caught, recorded, and reacted to.

Today's loosely coupled world of Web services, databases, and "virtual offices" also create the need for flexible, survivable processes. The technical process team must plan for failures.

There is a financial impact to process failures. Each process failure has an associated cost. Costs also increase as failures are hidden and the documentation and control are unstructured.

BPMN provides a powerful approach to managing failures in the form of exceptions and compensations. The exception shapes and compensations allow continuous operation throughout intermittent error conditions. For instance, some older applications use a manual process for the exception flow. This might be an outcome of the focus on "happy day" paths. Manual processes promote staff improvisations and undocumented "work arounds."

Figure 5–7 presents an example of BPMN's modeling of survivable processes in the survey pattern. If an error occurs in the email-reading process, it can be posted to a log and systems administrators can respond. The survey can continue. The process can loop back or complete.

The aim of BPMN is to support "long-running" transactions. For instance, a process-oriented car rental agency might create one process for each vehicle. In this case, the process could run for years.

Three Error Types

There are three types of exceptions that may affect process execution:

- Technical exceptions—the process server has failed.
- Transient exceptions—a needed resource for the process is unavailable.
- Business exceptions—the condition of the process is in error. Data is incomplete or has errors.

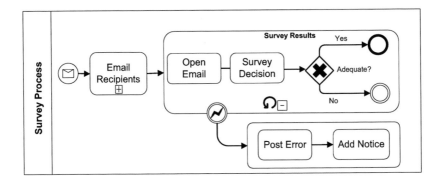

Figure 5–7   *BPMN for an exception in the survey process.*

Unfortunately, there is no cure or notation for the technical exception. When the server halts, recovering processes are dependent on the technical nature of the process server.

Decisions, supported by business rules, can create named business exceptions. If the process is transactional, the process should compensate for transactions that fail to complete. In compensation, the process cleans up or backs out records from ERPs, operational data stores, or data warehouses.

Processes often must be completed within a specific time period, so there could be time-out actions noted on the diagram. Business processes usually receive a message and translate that message into yet another message for consumption by the next part of the process. BPMN is powerful for developing time-outs, exceptions, and compensations. As described in Chapter 2, "BPMN: Basics and Gateways," you can attach time-outs, exceptions, and compensations directly to a subprocess task list. When time-outs and exceptions occur within the two process tasks, the process server traps these at the point of the subprocess.

Figure 5–8 presents a simple process server "architecture" for understanding the three types of errors. If the process server fails, then the process obviously cannot run and a technical error occurs. If the database service fails, then the process cannot get the data it needs to complete. This is a transient error. You should be able to restart the process instance and complete it once the database is restored. Users send data for the process in application servers. If users send incorrect data, then a business exception has occurred. Finally, you use process steps to resolve the error.

You can model business processes with advanced abilities that suspend processing or communicate with disconnected, mobile processes. They can add new technology, such as RFID. These powers yield opportunities for the enterprise to fine tune their most complicated practices. Yet, to develop these capabilities, you should understand how BPM tools use the three types of exceptions and what you must plan for when developing the production version of the process diagram.

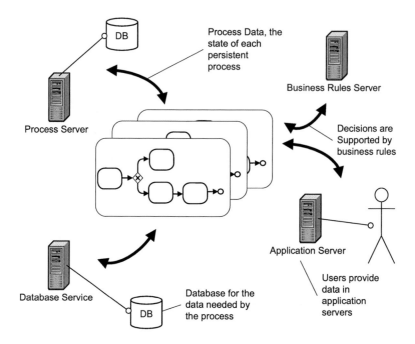

Figure 5–8   *Simplistic architecture for a process environment.*

A process diagram should use exception handlers to redirect the process flow when a transient or business exception happens. No one process, however, can manage every exception. There are technical exceptions that will cause the entire process instance to suspend.

Technical Exceptions

Technical exceptions occur when the process causes the Business Process Management System (BPMS) instance to fail. An internal server exception should be abnormal—however, there are operational circumstances that cause these. Technical exceptions include

- Exceptions caused by Illegal argument exceptions (suppose the process software changes an internal field from 20 to 10 characters).
- Process server database exceptions, "out of tablespace," violation of database constraints.

These are outside and therefore invisible to the calling subprocess. Processes cannot handle them because the execution state of the server has stopped. When this technical exception happens, the current transaction is always marked for rollback. The process throws the exception to the scheduler or message router.

Transient Exceptions

A transient exception is usually caused by servers external to the process server, like database connections or connection pooling exceptions. Within the scope of the current transaction, a transient exception is visible and the process can catch it with an exception handler. If the exception is not handled in the scope of the current transaction, the subprocess marks the transaction for rollback and throws the exception to the scheduler or message router. The process is suspended.

The suspended process can be restarted and resume processing after the database connection or some other condition is restored.

Business Exception

A business exception is one that can be expected by the process. Examples of these exceptions include

- Data in a process not being in the proper arrangement; users putting it in the wrong account.
- Exception raised by an activity—a specific, named exception is raised. For instance, a business rule could raise a named exception.

If the exception is not handled in the scope of the current activity, the activity fails. When the activity defines a coordinated transaction, the transaction is committed. When no exception handling takes place, exception processing begins and leads to compensation and the failure of the process.

Business Rules Decisions and Business Exceptions

As shown in Figure 5–8, you might use a business rules server to decide propositions about data in the process (the business rules server might be part of the process engine). These propositions include validations and transformations. A validation is verification of the truth of data in the process. A transformation assigns a data attribute, such as a customer discount. Both are important types of *decisions* that a business process makes with the data within process flows.

Evaluating the data in a set of transactions is a common decision pattern. Each record that fails the validation should be stored in an area for later clean up. You can either handle the validation directly, with values in the process flows, or you can raise a business exception, create a reusable process for handling the exception, and move on. Another common decision pattern validates user form input in a workflow. Users might correctly complete a form and send it to a process flow. If there are business rules that violate complex data and business conditions, the process should collect data from the user at a later date.

A decision service might validate incoming data. If the data does not pass validation, the subprocess raises a named exception—otherwise, the record is processed.

The basic idea is to design your exceptions, time-outs, and compensations to enlarge the flexibility of the process and allow most processes to continue unattended. Handle the process exception and move on.

Diagram Complexity

The integration or service-phase business process diagram has many important timing, compensation, and exception features. Unfortunately, these added boxes and notations make it difficult for business users to understand. Hopefully, the process phases and workflow modeling diagrams will be adequate. As details for error planning are added, you might need to create separate "views" of the process for the business and technical staff. Some BPM diagramming tools allow users to disable the display of exceptions, compensations, and timers attached to subprocesses. The tasks following these are not displayed. This clarifies the core nature of the process created in the early part of the process modeling effort.

SUMMARY

In the last two phases of the PMF, process designers coordinate the processes with patterns and plan for exceptions and errors.

You can speed up and improve your process modeling by adopting the patterns we discussed or creating your own standards for process patterns. We discussed three powerful patterns for coordinating workflows:

- Looping approval—the process participant is presented with a request and approves, denies, or requests more information.

- Surveys, marketing, and feedback—we request information from an unknown number of process participants and amass the response.

- Coordinating many choices—a process participant requests work be assigned to one of many resources in a queue.

As the BPM industry matures, more patterns will emerge. There are three types of exceptions:

1. Technical exceptions—errors that cause the server to crash.

2. Transient exceptions—a requested resource and condition is temporarily unavailable.

3. Business exception—a business rule has been violated.

CHAPTER 6

CONCLUSION

EVOLVING FROM FLOWCHARTS
AND WORKFLOW DIAGRAMS

Since the 1930s, business analysts have used flowcharts to describe processes. These largely industrial approaches spawned the workflow diagrams of the 1960s. Legacy flowchart and workflow diagramming approaches are still in widespread use. These techniques focus on mission-level "lines of control" and "areas of responsibility." The origins and outcomes are documentation of "batch-oriented" processes for "command-and-control" management. The systems they spawned, if any, were the stovepipes everyone wishes to expel.[1] Modeling business processes with BPMN changes the focus from macrolevel organization to more atomic objectives or goals. For instance, a process might describe the life cycle of an asset such as a truck or factory robot rather than the mission of the maintenance or manufacturing division.

The focus of legacy flowcharts and workflow diagrams is to define areas of responsibility. Workflows often focus on many objectives. They do not model a process as a transaction or assign the process to the participant. Their decision points do not model the perspective of the responsible person and they make no distinction between business rules and decision gateways. Because there is no distinction between a sequence and message flow, communication is not adequately atomic to identify inefficiencies. Without good discovery in a goal-focused way, inefficiencies will be hidden.

BPMN evolved from other diagram types and has some shapes in common, but a BPMN process diagram can show more detail than a flowchart. It documents who performs the tasks, in what order, and in what timeframe with activ-

---

1. A stovepipe is an old computer application so tightly bound together that the individual elements upgraded. The stovepipe system must be maintained until it can be entirely replaced.

ities performed by other participants. Processing steps for multiple process participants can be shown in the same diagram. Communication (interactions) can be plainly documented.

As BPMN becomes widely adopted, legacy flowchart approaches will fade. The process improvements of Six Sigma and Lean break down barriers by identifying unnecessary activities that move batches of data or work, and cede or assume responsibilities. BPMN diagrams describe process interactions as a large, long-running transaction. Defining these transactions, especially with a Lean mindset, moves the modeling focus to the process goal and highlights the barriers.

Beyond Six Sigma or Lean, other factors are driving process change in business and government. Regulations such as SOX and Basle II have created new processes. Best practices, including ITIL and COBIT, create still more. The outcome is a world that has become process-focused. Because message and transition are critical, legacy flowcharting techniques cannot model this complexity. BPMN is a more accurate and theoretically-sound modeling tool.

Unless the objective or goal of process modeling is clear, documenting complex business processes that involve multiple people, systems, policies, regulations, and other processes can be challenging. If you have used the old diagram styles, you need new skills with BPMN diagramming. The key to clear models is a focus on the process goal with proper diagram style. Good style includes consistent process layout. A BPMN diagram should read from left to right, top to bottom. Drawing a sequence flow from the right side of the diagram back to somewhere in the left of the diagram is referred to as "back edges." This is a legacy of the older styles of workflow diagrams where loop-back problems were modeled with "back-edge lines." The BPMN specification allows back edges, but we do not recommend them. There is a clearer way to draw this. A looping subprocess shows "back edges" without forcing the reader to follow lines going in every direction.

Sequence flows and messages (or signals) are a key modeling idea in BPMN. Message interactions show participant-to-participant communication in BPMN, while sequence flow signals a transition from one participant's task to the next.

We return to the supplier relationship management process first discussed in the introduction. Imagine that a process modeling group is working on a request for contract revisions at the PMF scenario level. The goal of the process is to manage the approval of contract revisions. Naturally, the business conversations concern people activities—contract administrators and managers. The process in Figure 6–1 transitions from the Contract Administrator's "Submit Contract" step back to the Manager''s "Review Contract" step. The first step to a better model would depict several participant pools. The next step would replace the "back-edge lines" with repeating steps that update original information.

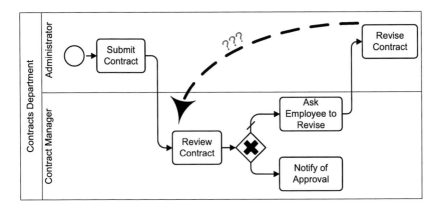

Figure 6–1   *A vague diagram in BPMN. Back edges go back in time in an awkward way*

The diagram in Figure 6–1 is poorly drawn for the following reasons:

- There are two participants in a pool. The symbol shows only one participant who has both a manager and contract administrator role.
- The ideas of task transition and interaction were not included in this diagram .
- Sequence flow is easiest to read when it progresses in a timeline. A loop-back should be contained in a scope (subprocess).
- The unifying theme is missing—the contract revision is buried in the messages.

We have some suggestions for a BPMN approach.

SCENARIO DIAGRAMMING WITH THE
PROCESS-ORIENTED APPROACH

Communication in BPMN should be modeled message interaction. Usually one participant or entity drives (or is the focus of) the process. In process modeling, you identify the process focus and the role the participant performs in the process. For instance, if the process deals with fleet maintenance, there should be a vehicle participant. If the process is an invoice, then there should be an invoice or invoice system participant.

There are several steps to clarifying the focus of the Figure 6–1 process. Figure 6–2 considers the timeline of activity for each participant. The interactions between participants are shown clearly, yet the point of the process is vague. In this example, the contract manager is clearly the originator of the contract revision

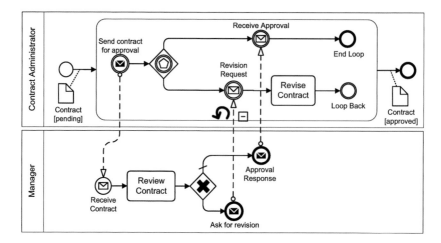

Figure 6–2   *Participants properly arranged into pools. The process is improved but the unifying idea is missing.*

approval process. In contrast, the manager performs a more passive role, responding to change requests.

A back-edge might imply that we want to go back in time and start over. The looping subprocess removes back-edges, or the "line back in time." Iterations of a looping subprocess each have an implicit scope for process data. A back-edge drawing has only one scope for data, so there is no way to separate original data from revisions. Rather than overwriting data, loop iterations add information.

This process starts when the contract administrator decides to send some information to a manager. The contract administrator then waits for one of two events to occur. Either the contract administrator receives an approval notice, or he is asked to revise his submission. After the revision is made, the subprocess loops back to the step that sends the contract revision to the manager.

Processes should show the perspective of the role being performed and the scope of the involvement. From the manager's perspective, the process starts with the "contract revision" message. After the message, the manager reviews the contract information and decides to either approve or reject. When the message is approved, the manager replies to the contract administrator with a warning; when rejected, a revision request is sent to the contract administrator. At this point, the manager's involvement ends. It is then the responsibility of the contract administrator participant to complete the process. Because the manager's involvement has ended, the manager will never know if the administrator does nothing. The example in Figure 6–2 includes no provision for a warning to the manager for the administrator's lack of action.

Process optimization involves analyzing diagrams for inefficiencies. Bottlenecks might be spotted in a well-formed diagram without simulation tools. In

Figure 6–2, the Contract Administrator cannot complete the contract revision if a manager needs excessive time reviewing the contract revisions. This is only one process instance. The contract administrator might revise dozens of contracts. The manager might be an approver for other processes besides the contract revision. The fact that there is no time-out warning for the manager suggests there is room for improving performance.

Processes achieve goals and should have a focus that orchestrates the interactions of the people participants. As mentioned in Chapter 4, "Gathering Requirements with BPMN," the goal of Figure 6–2's process is to complete Contract Revisions so the focus is on the Contract Revision. For instance, assume the contract revision arrives in an email. A paper document handed from one person to the next is reliable, but email can be unreliable. Servers might introduce lengthy message delivery delays. Widely used spam filters block important information without warning. Therefore, Figure 6–2 needs another participant—the process participant.

Orchestrating System and Human Participants

Digitizing a process with a Business Process Management System (BPMS) is the goal of most process modeling activities. Before a process can be digitized, it must be properly modeled. Process diagrams document the application architecture. A good process design carefully considers all participants—people, systems, and other processes. As often occurs, the contract revisions process starts with a people-to-system interaction. In this way, computer systems are process participants, too. Examples of system participants include software applications, email servers, ERP systems, and websites. Failure to recognize the system participant might lead to inefficiencies.

The process participant manages the messaging interaction between people and systems. This is an abstraction of all system interaction. Technical diagrams such as the PMF integration and services show direct system interaction, but in a scenario diagram we focus on the business participants. Showing technical details at this level might distract a reader from the business objective. The new participant assumes the responsibility for managing the interactions with all the systems. The diagram in Figure 6–2 includes the focus of the design effort—the contract revision process participant. It correctly manages messages routing from the Contract Administrator to the Manager. The Contract Administrator starts the process, but flow control of the process is the responsibility of the contract revisions process participant.

At the PMF scenario level, we recommend modeling how the focus of the process interacts with people. Scenario-level diagrams should not show too many details, and Figure 6–3 does not show the full complexity of a digitized process. The scenario diagram reflects the expertise of business analysts and SMEs. The process flow of the system at a technical level can be shown in another diagram, such as the PMF integration or services diagram.

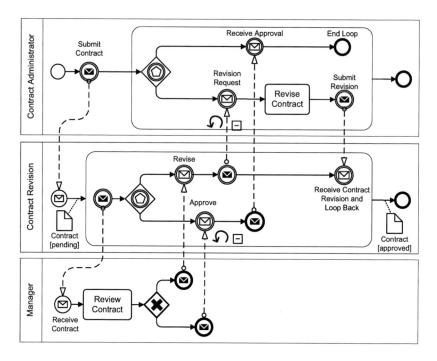

Figure 6–3   *Adding a system participant called Contract Revision for partial automation.*

Modeling with the Goal of Automation

Diagramming interactions with a process participant focus efficiently reveals important details about the interaction. This style of BPMN diagram is easily converted into a digitized process. In the example, we identified a Contract Revision task as the focus of the modeling process. Contract Revisions is the focus of the digitized process and is referred to as the "process participant." The process participant keeps knowledge of each interaction and every activity state.

The process participant might collectively represent the entire contract negotiations department. As the process becomes digitized, a BPMS can orchestrate the messaging between participants. Gateway conditions are evaluated by the BPMS, based on message data sent from other participants.

As shown in Figure 6–4, one approach to process modeling is to begin with the process participant and progressively add participants, activities, and gateways from the perspective of the process objective. After you have identified the interaction points for the process participant, it is easy to add another participant and draw more interaction lines. So, model your process from a "process participant" approach first. This will show a clear sequence of activities and events.

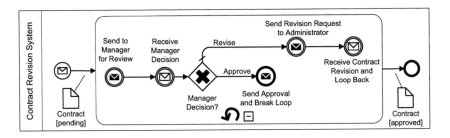

Figure 6–4 *Use a single pool for analyzing the scenario.*

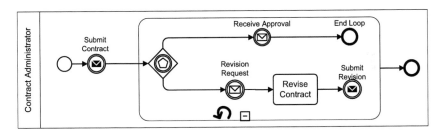

Figure 6–5 *Diagramming each participant's perspective individually.*

Next, identify the participants and place them in a pool. Model each participant individually, each interacting only with the process participant. Use the phrase "from the perspective of this participant." For example,

- "From the perspective of the accounting department...the contract revision" (this adds an accounting department).
- "From the perspective of the submitting contract administrator ... the contract revision."
- "From the perspective the of the approving managers ... the contract revision."

As you add participants, you progressively capture the scenario. As shown in Figure 6–5, this modeling strategy yields more accurate diagrams because all steps required to complete a process are recognized first.

The contract administrator's perspective is a bit different. After a submission is made, the contract administrator receives one of two possible events. Either a notice is received stating the contract revision was approved, or a request for revision is received. To break a loop, you typically should use the empty End event, unless you are trying to express error conditions.

As shown in Figure 6–6, the manager's perspective on the process is even simpler. The Manager role's job is to get a contract revision request, approve it,

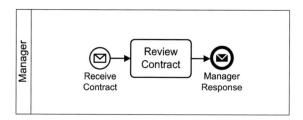

Figure 6–6   *The manager's perspective.*

and pass it back to the process. The automation portion of the process makes all the routing decisions for you, so the Manager role does not have to have any specific knowledge of with which participant to communicate.

You could argue that the Manager is also in a loop, but the Manager's process ends. The Manager will reprocess the entire request when it is resubmitted. If the manager is involved in the revision, then this is a different scenario and requires another interaction between manager and the process participant.

When you put all of these process pools together, it looks something like that shown in Figure 6–8. Now you have a process that captures the full involvement of all participants.

THE MANUAL PROCESS APPROACH

There are still processes in the world that are not digitized and may not be for some time. Documenting the "as is" scenario is valuable in understanding how the digitized process will impact your organization. Let's take a look how the absence of the process automation system affects our diagramming.

With no automation system involved, we have to decide who or what (which participant) is driving this process. Finally, it's the manager who hires the employee and tells him to get to work. The employee produces the work and sends it to the manager (Figure 6–7).

Throughout this entire process, the Employee participant is driving the work, and the Manager performs a service role, where it simply responds to requests from the Employee participant. The decisions are being made by the Manager participant, however, and the Employee participant simply responds to the Manager action.

In summary, whether you chose the system participant or the manual approach, breaking the process into participants, activities, and events is useful. Choose a participant that owns or is the focus of the process. Model what they do. Put yourself in his shoes and discover how he sees the process. The points of interaction will be easier to spot once each perspective is accurately depicted. When you have completed the "as is" process model, opportunities for optimization might be easily spotted in patterns.

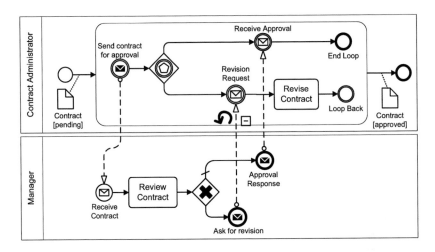

Figure 6–7   *A manual process that has no systems as a participant.*

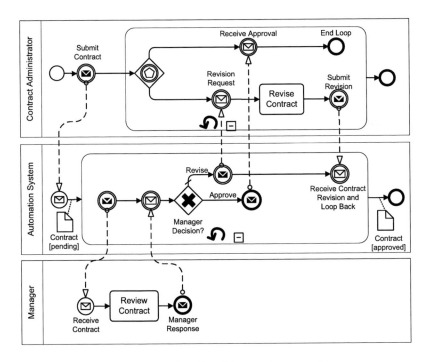

Figure 6–8   *All perspectives combined and interacting properly.*

TECHNICAL BPMN DIAGRAMS—
PMF SERVICES AND INTEGRATIONS

BPMN is a succinct notation for business and technical processes. BPMN combines features from Unified Modeling Language (UML) and traditional flowchart diagrams. UML is a precise, fine-grained modeling tool and it has a rich and complicated notation. BPMN requires fewer diagrams for systems programming. BPMN also lessens written documentation. In text, a BPMN diagram's written functions might span many pages, an improvement over UML and written process requirements. Because it is a common language for business and IT, BPMN is a rapidly growing process documentation tool.

Processes specified by BPMN diagrams improve the understanding of business stakeholders. IT engineers and architects clearly communicate business process and business decisions, so the roles of IT staff and business analysts are balanced.

In the Process Modeling Framework (PMF), discussed in the introduction, some processes should be owned by the IT department. These (particularly the ITIL[1] variety) are used by business processes. BPMN is a good choice for documenting enterprise-wide processes.

Having a good plan is efficient when you start building a project. For example, before construction begins on a new building, a blueprint that precisely positions wiring, plumbing, and ventilation is necessary. A construction plan places each part of a skyscraper in a certain order. First the foundation is laid, and then the frame is erected. Internal walls and ceilings are installed last. You could build a building without any equipment, and then later install the wiring, plumbing, and ventilation. But consider the repeated efforts that would be required. Walls and ceilings would need to be patched. Retrofitting might also compromise the integrity of the structure. This analogy helps explain why the PMF is important to business process development. In process modeling, you create specialized business processes for your organization. Creating an executable process should include a blueprint of the structure and a well-crafted plan for construction. The BPMN diagrams serve as the blueprint, and the PMF serves as the plan for construction.

A technical BPMN diagram not only serves as a construction plan; it is also valuable when making changes and diagnosing problems ("as is" documents). Blueprints for a skyscraper are helpful to an architect when remodeling a floor for a new tenant. Without a schematic diagram for an electronic circuit, repair would be nearly impossible. Collections of well-crafted BPMN diagrams help an organization manage business processes when making changes or diagnosing efficiency problems.

---

1. Information Technology Infrastructure Library

There is plenty of commercial software that converts BPMN diagrams into executable code. The BPMN specification maps directly to Java, Business Process Execution Language (BPEL), or other languages. As the business community accepts BPMN over flowcharts, BPMN will improve understanding and reduce the size of requirements documents. By reducing IT staff resources, the time saved can be better used in creating services and integrations.

Modern process automation involves assembling a set of prebuilt parts in a logical order to achieve a business goal. Each part is well-tested and documented, and comes with a standard interface. This standard interface is driven by the SOA governance strategies. Increasingly, the standard documentation for SOA is BPMN.

Integration Diagrams

There are many terms used for integration diagrams. Some examples include "services orchestration," "BPM in the small," and "interface layer." All three of these examples accurately describe an integration diagram. An integration diagram is small, and it orchestrates services. It also acts as a standard interface between a scenario and a service.

Integration diagrams should include error handling, compensation, and transactions. All services have the potential for error conditions. Working with multiple data, stores might need a transaction with compensation for activity rollback.

The life cycle of an integration process might be a matter of seconds. This is referred to as "short-running." At the most, integration processes might complete within a few hours. Because the lifecycle is short, an integration process might use a bidirectional (synchronous) message instead of two separate (asynchronous) messages.

The short lifecycle allows an integration process to be updated without concern for long-running instances. Stuck services can easily be detected with a timer event on the subprocess. The timer event might escalate to an IT administrator. This is an ideal pattern for managing an SOA environment.

IMPORTANT VENDORS

TIPPING POINT SOLUTIONS

Tom Debevoise is the Chief Technology Officer and cofounder of Tipping Point Solutions, Inc. His blog can be found at *www.tomdebevoise.com.*

Tipping Point offers a full line of training options in business modeling in BPMN, including the material in this book. Tipping Point has also integrated training in business process modeling with the business rules approach.

From management and economic theories to technical architectures, many ideas offer the promise of creating a perfect realm for businesses competing in today's globally-networked world. They often tout the means to "close the gap" between management strategies and technical or operational means, yet the barrier is still demanding. Tipping Point's mission is to empower and enable firms with disruptive technology. Empowerment arises from increasing a firm's maturity in business processes, decisions, and business rules. To achieve this, Tipping Point offers a proven catalog of methods, training, and consulting services.

Tipping Point's leadership provides critical practices and approaches for achieving agility across the entire enterprise, from the perspective of BPM and the Business Rules Approach. This includes business tactics, changing requirements, enterprise architecture, software, and methodologies. Tipping Point presents its customers with the BPM and decision management approach to the planning, management, and operational actions that are needed to achieve business agility. We help enterprises create processes that are not merely technically agile, but also business agile.

Tipping Point Solutions, Inc. has extensive experience delivering strategic technology services to the commercial market space. Tipping Point solutions empowers organizations to maintain strategic control and governance over their processes and decisions. Tipping Point's approach to process improvement solutions is different than the conventional approach for business re-engineering.

Our approach is to look at an enterprise's business models, promote integrative thinking, and deploy tactical, low-cost solutions that never lose sight of business agility needs. Deployment advances at an incremental cadence so as to heighten the short-term return on investment while keeping the strategic picture in focus.

In addition to training and mentoring, Tipping Point is creator of the SOA libretto—the only vendor-neutral comprehensive process, rules intelligence SOA methodology available.

To read more about Tipping Solutions, Inc., please visit *www.tipping-point.net.*

INTALIO SOFTWARE

Rick Geneva is a process expert with Intalio Software. If you are interested in entering and executing a business process in BPMN then you should consider trying Intalio Software—the leading Open Source Business Process Management Suite (BPMS) vendor. Intalio has granted its BPMS server to the Apache foundation and its BPMN modeler to the Eclipse STP Project. A continuing effort to promote Open Source continues through its community at *http://bpms.intalio.com.* A special website, *www.intalio.org,* lists these projects.

Business Process Management is the service-oriented architecture killer application. Intalio helps over 10,000 organizations around the world get the highest return on investment from their SOA efforts. Highest return is achieved when working with hard, lengthy, and intricate processes—it simplifies complex processes. Intalio focuses on giving you the tools for tough business problems—the ones that can include thousands of steps—including a dependencies tool, run-time versioning, enterprise-class clustering, and support for stateful exchange protocols.

With Intalio, you design, revise, and deploy new business processes without having to write one line of code. One BPMN box replaces 10 lines of BPEL code that, in turn, replaces 100 lines of J2EE code. Code is bad for agility. Your business flexibility is held back by debugging and IT staff backlog. With graphical development, your staff is in control. Intalio's BPMS dramatically reduces your direct development cost and at the same time affords you the needed business agility for real process innovation.

It is operation-system agnostic, supports the latest BPMN 1.1, BPEL 2.0, and BPEL4PEOPLE standards. This is essential for interoperability, and necessary for intricate and sophisticated processes. The designer is based on the Eclipse framework, the server is based on Geronimo, and both are cross-platform. For special requirements, Intalio offers its innovative Demand Driven Development. This allows the outsourced development of special features.

Founded in July 1999, Intalio is a privately held, venture-backed company in Palo Alto, California. For more information on Intalio, please call 650-596-1800 or visit *www.intalio.com.*

INDEX